TRADING ASHES FOR BEAUTY

God's Answer for Those of a Wounded
Spirit

By

Pastor Nathaniel Jones

ISBN – 978-0-9748811-9-5

Published By: New Life Publishing
P.O. Box 210891
Dallas, Texas 75211
1-866-602-2672
www.newlifepublishing.biz

Cover Designed By – S. Davis

Printed in the United States of America

TABLE OF CONTENTS

INTRODUCTION:

Understanding Beauty and Ashes

NOTE: As you read sections VIII (Don't Blame God) and X (Misunderstanding the Sovereignty of God); please do so with an open spirit mind and meditate on the scriptures found in those writings.

Dedication

I dedicate this writing and work to my parents, John L. Jones and Almeda Jones. Though they have both gone home to be with Jesus, they were responsible for releasing me as a seed in the Earth and gave me the opportunity to grow and develop. When I was a young boy at the age of nine years old and the threat of death was on me in a hospital room, my mother gave me back to the Lord. Without my parents' contribution there would be no Nathaniel Jones.

Also to my sister, Loletta Wynder, who after the death of our parents continued to carry the torch of leadership for our family and holding us together. I love you, "Lo."

Special Thanks

I want to thank my lovely wife, Patricia Ann Jones, for her contribution to this work. Her commitment and dedication as a wife helped me stay the course and finish what I started. She never complained all the nights and days I worked on this project, but rather she prayed for me. Patricia has been there when I had the opportunity to be bitter due to offense; she encouraged me to get better and not bitter. Thank you, Sweetheart.

Thanks to my sons, Jonathan A. Jones, Bradley Jerome Nash and Nathaniel Jones, Jr. Having three strong-willed sons will teach any father about prayer and staying focused on Christ. Thank you, boys.

I want to thank the Students for Christ Ministry at Southern University in Baton Rouge, LA. It was a Bible study group that existed when I went to college during the years of 1976 through 1980. We were a bunch of baby Christians that learned how to serve God through much trials and persecution. Thanks to my teachers and mentors: Charles Allen, Harold Alexander, Ricky Andrews, Wesley Crawford, Bill Moody, the late Leonard Royal, Dorothy Washington Muldrow and Tony Wesley. It was brothers and sisters such as these who helped me in my beginning years of ministry to develop character and gifts. I will always be grateful to my humble beginnings.

Special thanks to my brother, Dr. Kenneth Wayne Jones. Over the years we've been closer that Jonathan and David. He has encouraged my heart and stood by me through difficult times. It is love and companionship like that which I greatly value. Thank you, Ken.

I'm thankful to my local church, Greater First Baptist Church, in Bartlesville, OK, and Dr. Timothy Jackson, pastor and friend, who has welcomed this Gift of an Apostle in his church without intimidation or fear. He has freely allowed Patricia and me to operate and help strengthen the church.

Special thanks to Laurie Connolly, who made this project possible by her love and compassionate help. I trust God will give her the desires of her heart.

Thank you, Jesus, for saving this Catholic boy in 1976 and bringing him into the Kingdom of God for such a time as this. You allowed me to endure the pain of divorce in order that I might understand being wounded. You gave me grace to forgive those who wounded me and you healed those whom I inflicted injury upon. Now that I have been converted, I want to strengthen the brethren.

The ability to preach, teach, and expound upon scripture comes from the anointing of the Holy

Spirit. Without the call of God on my life I could do nothing, nor would I be anything. Thank you, Jesus.

INTRODUCTION:

"For I am poor and needy, and my heart is wounded within me." Psalms 109:22

It has been said that the most dangerous animal of any type is a wounded animal. The rationale behind this statement says when you approach a healthy, unharmed animal you approach with caution in defense mode knowing that it might over power you and that its intent is to hurt you.

However, when you approach a wounded animal your attitude is one in which you make yourself vulnerable and your defense mechanisms are lowered because you don't expect a wounded animal to strike back, but rather welcome your assistance. Whether you are trying to free him from a hunter's trap and you're attempting to bandage a broken limb, you are making yourself vulnerable. You are putting yourself at risk.

On the other hand, in the animal's mind it is thinking you're coming to finish it off as you take advantage of their wounded body. So the wounded animal musters up one last courageous fight to defend itself. As you slowly move in to assist (with no plan to further harm it) the animal (victim) is defensive and it will spring into self defense mode and will attempt to kill you. When this happens you ask yourself, "What did I do wrong, I was only trying to help?"

This is the case with many who have tried to help wounded people. A phrase was coined by someone wiser than myself and it is this, *"Hurting people, hurt people."* It is a simple truth that packs a lot of power. Professional counselors, psychologists and those in the helping profession need to understand that people who have been hurt emotionally, traumatized, belittled by life's pressures, abused and suffocated by guilt don't readily recognize that their efforts are being made to assist them, but they are afraid that those individuals (counselors/ministers) are there to harm them. Wounded and hurting people often reject the helping hands of others.

Proverbs 18:14 says, "The strong spirit of a man will sustain him in bodily pain or trouble but a weak and broken spirit who can raise up or bear?" (Amplified Bible)   Life can be cruel and unfair to men and many times the constant trials of life can cause many wounds. The strongest individual can have his/her spirit crushed and fall prey to the unfortunate injuries to the human soul. A strong spirit man will help us to stand on God's Word for healing and believing for financial needs to be met, but a wounded spirit makes it difficult to receive God's peace and soundness of mind. It takes the loving power of God to reach into the inner recesses of our soul to administer healing and restoration.   It is God's design that we be made whole: spirit, soul and body. You can be the healthiest person in the world and have great knowledge of scripture, but if your soul (emotional state) is destroyed you are not a whole person.

The purpose of this writing is to address the dangers of a wounded spirit and give God's remedies through His loving hands that will *turn your ashes into beauty*. Jesus declared that part of His earthy ministry was to heal the broken hearted, preach deliverance to the captives and set at liberty those that have been bruised (Luke 4:18). Scripture says that the Lord is near those that are of a broken heart and contrite spirit (Psalms 34:18). There is healing for your brokenness. Whether you are a victim of a broken home, bad divorce, horrific sexual abuse, abandonment or church maltreatment, Jesus is the healing balm of Gilead (Jeremiah 8:22).

13

It is the will of God that you overcome your unpromising past and emotional scars and to live a life of cheerful anticipation. You can truly, *"just get over it."* Jesus said, "be of good cheer, I've overcome the world and its problems (John 16:33). As a believer in Christ, He has taken up resident within your life and spirit and declares that, "Greater is He that is living in you than he (satan) that is in the world". (I John 4:4)

Faith and confidence in God will give you strength to overcome the injuries of your past life and give you courage and strength to face tomorrow with a smile (I John 5:4). The same God that you trust to heal your broken body of cancer, heart disease, high blood pressure, etc., is the same God that can and will heal your broken heart. The same application of faith is to be used to receive healing for your wounded spirit.

You will not find a bunch of psychological or mental health jargon in this writing. Nor will this writing include psychological therapy or techniques to soothe your conscience. Those in the mental health profession can only put a bandage on the cancerous sores of emotional trauma that has left many on the road side as road kill. However, you will receive from this teaching the promises of God (who cannot lie) that will heal your broken heartedness. I want you to understand that God will deliver you from the captive hands of satan, giving you a hope and a future (Jeremiah 29:11-14).

Allow the spiritual revelations within these pages to give you confidence of your Father's love that will chase away the sleepless nights and emptiness of your dying soul. You can trade your ashes in for beauty and wear God's forgiveness like a crown of righteousness. What an exchange that God offers. He tells us to give Him our broken heart and He will give up abundant life. We can know love, joy and peace in our lives as rivers of living waters with an endless supply. Why not give Jesus all your shattered dreams, wounded hearts and fading hopes. He will turn your sorrow into joy. Will you trust Him today? Don't try Jesus, but trust Him.

Understanding Beauty and Ashes

*Isaiah 61:1-3 "The Spirit of the Lord God is upon me; because the Lord hath anointed me to preach good tiding unto the meek; He hath sent me to bind up the brokenhearted, to proclaim liberty to the captives, and the opening of the prison to them that are bound. To proclaim the acceptable year of the Lord, and the day of vengeance of our God; to comfort all that mourn; To appoint unto them that mourn in Zion, to give unto them **beauty for ashes**, the oil of joy for mourning, the garment of praise for the spirit of heaviness; that they might be called trees of righteousness, the planting of the Lord, that He might be glorified.*

In the Bible days, throwing ashes upon one's head symbolized an outward sign of inward distress, pain and hopeless. The ashes represented human frailty (Genesis 18:27 & Job 30:19), humiliation (Job 42:6, Psalms 102:9) and mourning (II Samuel 13:19 & Esther 4:1-3). Life's trauma and circumstances can cause much human suffering, humiliation and pain. We could find ourselves going through long periods of mourning, grief and sorrow due to injury, loss and betrayal. Wounds cut deep into our soul and life seems to continue to add salt into those wounds keeping them bleeding and open to further infection.

Mourning is an expression of showing pain, grief and sorrow. In the Bible, death was often associated with weeping, tearing off clothing and putting on sackcloth and ashes. A period of mourning could last seven days and sometimes a professional mourner was paid to help (Mark 5:40).

It was also an expression of grief over sin and repentance.

Satan wants to exploit our pain and cause us to blame God or others for our pain. He (satan) wants us to internalize our pain and not trust in the power of God to make us whole. Man is a threefold being: spirit, soul and body. If either one of the individual entities are disturbed or broken, satan has a foothold to enter and disrupt God's plan for our wholeness, wellness and soundness. Emotional trauma can cause irreparable damages in our soul that could eventually affect our spirit. When our spirit and soul are affected it could cause our bodies to be damaged as well in the form of sickness and disease. Jesus came that you might have abundant life in every area of your life.

The great exchange is that God wants to trade your ashes for beauty. God's beauty is cheerful anticipation of a better life for you. Biblically speaking, the beauty represents a nuptial tiara (fancy headdress) instead of ashes thrown on the head while mourning. This headdress and garment of praise express praise and gratitude instead of mourning and a spirit of heaviness. God has promised that all that mourn in ashes will be clothed with comfort and the oil of joy. God has healing for your brokenness. Satan may have brought calamity in your life and caused you great pain, but God will pour in the oil and wine of His touch to make you whole. Accept His invitation to be made whole and be set free. Jesus' initial purpose was to come to give us life through His death, burial and resurrection, but His dying was not to be in vain. He wants us to trust Him to take the difficulties of every day life and use them as a stepping-stone to victorious living. Your ashes can be turned into a beautiful thing when you trust Him. He wants you to worship Him and turn your trial into a testimony.

Remember, "weeping may endure for a night, but joy comes in the morning." (Psalms 30:5b) Take on the whole armor of God and ready yourself for a battle. However, the battles is not yours but the Lord's (I Samuel 17:47). Life and trouble happen to us all, but we must trust in the Lord to deliver us and mend our broken hearts as we travel through life's trials. He will give you beauty for your ashes and cause you to be an ornament of His grace.

NOT BUILT FOR THIS

NOTE: God did not design you initially to suffer pain and heartache. He created you for His glory that knows no pain or the damages of a wounded spirit. Things changed with the sin of Adam. Keep reading.

In the beginning man was created by God to be a reflection of Himself in the Earth. Jesus said that when we pray, we should pray, "thy will be done on Earth as it is in Heaven." Our lives on the Earth should reflect the heavenly. Beloved, in Heaven God is not sad, depressed, traumatized, oppressed and not sorrowful of heart. Adam was created with the God-given ability to reign over the circumstances of life. He was told to be fruitful and multiply, replenish the Earth and subdue it and exercise dominion over it (Genesis 2:28). Adam was created to be more than a conqueror . When sin entered the Garden, Adam subjected all men to failure, pain and suffering. Romans 5:8-17

God's original mandate was for man to rule on Earth as He rules in the Heaven. When Adam sinned and committed high treason against God it opened the door to sin and death (Romans 5). Man was created to live forever. He was only introduced to death through sin. Eve was deceived but Adam knew what God had said. The mere fact that he did not protect his wife, symbolizes the failure of man not to protect their children and loved ones; leaving them a prey to satan. Satan is the one that comes to steal, kill and destroy. We will never enjoy abundant life promised to us by Jesus as long as we allow satan to raise his ugly head and penetrate our lives (John 10:10 and Revelations 12:11).

In Genesis 3:4, satan spoke a half truth to Eve. Satan said "ye shall not surely die." The part that was correct was that Adam and Eve would not die a physical death. He (satan) knows that God would not kill His creation once the declaration became law. However, God had to kill something, so He killed an animal and used the skins to clothe man's nakedness.

The death man experienced on that day was separation from God. Sin separates you from your position in God. God immediately instituted a redemptive plan that would reconnect man back to Him. He promised a Savior, Emmanuel, Redeemer and Comforter. His death, burial and resurrection would save men from their sins and man could once again have access to his God. He would have access to God's power, divine provisions and protection. Through the Born Again experience God could sustain man in his spirit and have fellowship with man like he had with Adam in the "cool of the day." (Genesis 3:8) Man could be reborn of the Spirit of God through Christ (II Corinthians 5:17-21).

__Man a Triune Being__

I Thessalonians 5:23 – *"And the God of peace sanctify you wholly and I pray your whole spirit, soul and body be preserved blameless unto the coming of the our Lord Jesus Christ."*

Man is a triune being. He has a threefold makeup of spirit, soul and body. God created <u>man as a spirit</u> (Genesis 1:27; John 4:24 and Hebrews 12:9), <u>he lives in a body</u> (I Corinthians 3:16, 16 and 6:19, 20) and <u>he possesses a soul</u> (James 1:21). The terms spirit and soul are interchangeable and you need to be able to rightly divide the Word of God to know when scripture is referring to our human spirit or our soul (mind – Hebrews 4:12 says the two can be separated). The soul is referring to man's reasoning, intellect, feelings, will and emotions. Your soul (mind) is the gateway to your spirit. You are fearfully and wonderfully made and God has wired you in a way that your mind is connected to your spirit. If you are not strong in your spirit man your thinking, emotions, reasoning and intellect can affect your spirit man. The wounded spirit is the same as a broken heart. It is the seat of your emotions and the core of man.

Remember this; your heart is the same as your soul. The term whole heart means that your spirit and soul are operating as one. This is the ultimate plan of God is that we serve Him with our whole heart. Your spirit is in communication with God and you are joined to Christ by the Holy Spirit. Your soul (heart, intellect, reasoning, emotions, will, etc.), _once renewed_, work with the spirit man to serve God holistically. Romans 12:1-3

The Bible tells us to renew our minds on the Word of God (Romans 12:1-3) and instructs us to cast down imaginations and negative thought patterns contrary to the Word of God (II Corinthians 10:1-5. The battleground of life is won or loss in the mind.

Satan can't get to your spirit so he attacks your mind. In reference to a wounded spirit, satan constantly brings up our past, seasoned with guilt, condemnation and the temptation of unforgiveness, hatred and anger. Sadly too many fall prey to satan's plan. We give place to the devil and walk in the works of the flesh – never forgiving, forbearing and being bitter (Ephesians 4:27-32).

Satan in his subtlety knows that if he can dominate your mind; feelings, emotions and passions of the hearts, he can control nearly every aspect of your life. Your spirit is saved and satan can't touch that. However, through life's circumstances that you witness with your eyes and experience through your emotions, he can make life so difficult that you will almost (some do) succumb and surrender to his will, making you a captive. His goal is to snuff out the life of God in you.

Good news! *God did not create you for fear, anxiety, unforgivenss and emotional pain.* There is a way out through the Cross of Christ. It is faith in that Name that gives you victory. If you are not challenged to accept God's way to victory yet, keep reading. Help is on the way.

Your body will respond negatively to the ills of life. Life deals some of us a bad hand and we have to play it regardless. Some of us put on a good poker face and appear to be willing to play its game, but we are the casualties of life's problems. Some of us put on that poker face and try to hide the pain, injury and despair we are feeling. Some of us act out our pain and spew out anger, rebellion and poisonous reactions that cause innocent people to get hurt. Those innocent victims had nothing to do with our past, but yet you punish them because you are wounded and hurt.

You weren't created by God to house and experience pain, worry, and emotional trauma. You were created to glorify God in your bodies and in

your spirits that are His (I Corinthians 6:19, 20).
The Bible says, "praise is comely for the upright"
(Psalms 33:1). We were created for worship and
praise God and anything else does not glorify God.
God has given a mandate to the believer to present
his body as a living sacrifice to God and to renew
their mind on the Word of God (Romans 12:1-3).
God's plan is for us to live an abundant live full of
love, joy and peace. Life struggles, orchestrated by
satan are sent to disrupt the plan of God and work in
conjunction with the thief that comes to steal, kill
and destroy. The Fruit of the Spirit represent the
life and character of Christ operating through our
recreated spirit (Galatians 5:22, 23). Any other
manifestations (works of the flesh – Galatians 5:19-
21) are contrary to the life and the plan of God for
your life. The works of the flesh respond to life's
trauma differently than the love of God that is in our
human spirit (Galatians 5:19-21). When we
respond in the flesh the results lead to
unforgiveness, bitterness, anger and hatred. These

responses further separate us from the peace, wholeness and soundness God has provided for us through His Son.

Your bodies have an adverse effect to worry, unforgiveness, bitterness, anger and anxiety. Professionals of the mental health field have documented proof that various stresses, anxieties and worries will affect your physical and mental health. <u>The reason for this is because God did not create you to worry, be anxious, unforgiving or bitter.</u> Such emotional trauma will affect your longevity of life and cause you to fail in human relationships that God has ordained for you to have with others. Most of our problems are associated with the mistreatment and betrayal at the hands of others, but yet God expects us to receive healing through our loving reactions (walking in forgiveness and forbearance) to those who hurt us.

God ordained for us to be loving, joyous and forgiving individuals that express His nature and love to others. Living out God's ordained purpose in human relationships is for us to breathe life and health to everyone that we come into human contact with. Too often we get hurt by trusting and extending a hand to others, however it does not change the plan of God. Jesus was persecuted and betrayed by those He came to save. Man was a wounded animal that Jesus came to rescue. The more Jesus came to help, the more He was rejected. Nevertheless, He gave His life for those that God ordained He should die for. This was the true love of God that all men secretly desire.

God knows that if you give life you will reap life (Galatians 6:7, 8). Brokenhearted people are like broken cisterns that cannot hold water (Jeremiah 2:12, 13). Those who have had their hearts broken cannot sustain the life of God in their lives. We are called to be rivers of living water, however there are those that represent the Dead Sea. They are dammed up like a dam with bitterness, hatred and unforgiveness. They neither have life and they cannot sustain life. God wants you healed of your wounded spirit so that He might use you for His glory to touch other lives and share His life with them.

The soul of man is the seat of emotions. Satan manipulates the circumstances of life to his advantage to separate men from God. It is our emotions that determine our passion for God and our level of spiritual growth in Him. If you have no passion for Christ you will not pray to Him daily, you will not worship Him and seek to grow in His Word. The enemy of our souls knows that if he can dominate our flesh, we cannot please God or glorify Him with our lives (Romans 8:1-14).

NOTE: The terms soul and spirit are interchangeable terms. We serve God out of our spirit man while our soul involves our intellect, reasoning, feelings, will and emotions. When we are told to present our bodies as a living sacrifice and we are told to renew our minds (soul), God is telling us that the threefold nature of man need to be on the same page following His mandates of scripture. The spirit man must be strong to overrule the will of our mind, which is our carnal flesh. Romans 8, tells us that the carnal flesh is against God's Word and is not subject to God's will for our lives. That is why we must renew our mind on the Word of God in order for it to work in conjunction with the spirit of man and the Spirit of God. The flesh (body) is neutral and will follow the most dominate one. Prayerfully, your dominate one, will be your spirit man and not your unrenewed mind.

Since the carnal mind is not subject to the will of God, satan will send unfortunate situations into your lives to get you to react carnally and disobey God. He (satan) wants us to react carnally and fleshly with feelings of unforgiveness, bitterness, hatred and strife. We can allow ourselves to respond according to God's Word or we can allow spiritual death to enter into our hearts, fleeing the commands of God.   Proverbs 4:20-23 says that we need to guard our hearts (soul) against such negative emotional responses because the issues of life proceed from our heart.   The heart is the seat of emotions and what you allow to get into your heart with come out to produce life or death.   Read Matthew 12:33-37 & 15:16-20

His (satan) goal is that you extend all your energies fighting through the murk and mire of emotional trauma so that we have little strength to live out of our spirit man for God.   Scriptures tells us that we wrestle not against flesh and blood, but against principalities and powers (satan demonic imps – Ephesians 6:10-12). *We need to stop fighting those that caused us pain and yield to the healing power of God, Almighty*. Isaiah 40:29- 31 says, *"He gives power to the tired and worn out, and strength to the weak. Even the youth shall be exhausted, and the young men will give up. But they that wait upon the*

Lord shall renew their strength. They shall mount up with wings like eagles; they shall run and not be weary, they shall walk and not faint." If you are brokenhearted or the victim of life's suffering and pain; wait on the Lord. He will change you from being a victim to a victor.

Proverbs 18:14 says, the strong spirit of a man will sustain him in bodily injury or trouble, but a weak and broken spirit (soul) who can raise up or bear. <u>I don't care how strong you are spiritually if your soul is not intact, satan will cause the unresolved issues of life that have caused you pain to lead to your demise.</u> You can stand on the Word of God and conquer in this life by Christ Jesus (Romans 8:37), but if you allow unforgiveness and bitterness to dominate your emotions (soul) you will be defeated on every hand.

Jesus told the leper that returned to give thanks that he was made whole (Luke 17:11-19). He made the same statement to blind Bartimaeus (Mark 10), the lady with the issue of blood (Mark 5) and the Syrophenician woman (of her daughter – Matthew 15). Why did he specifically use the term *'made whole?'* Each one of these individuals was treated poorly either by the community leaders, the rich, religious leaders, family and people in the neighborhood. Surely the Bartimaeus heard the rich criticize him, as he was a beggar. The lady with the issue of blood and the leper were rejected and considered outcast. The Syrophenician mother had to live with guilt and shame, as her daughter was not allowed to play with other children. Hearing the ridicule and hurtful statements, feeling the rejection and lack of love could cause anyone to have emotional scars and trauma. To complicate matters further they had a physical ailment in their bodies. Although Jesus told them they were healed in their physical bodies, if they did not forgive those that hurt them, they would not be able to sustain their healing. Unforgiveness, bitterness and hatred had to be repented of or satan would have a foothold to return and further inflict them. Being made whole is the ultimate goal of God for your life. Ten lepers were healed in Luke 17, but only one was made whole. Are you whole? Would you like to be made whole? Don't harbor hurt feelings or unforgiveness and you will be whole.

Moses' temper cost him dearly and stopped him from entering the Promised Land. Samson's lust for strange women cost him his sight and strength. He never truly fulfilled God's plan for his life. Judas' covetous spirit and unwillingness to repent led to his suicidal death. Proverbs 16:32, says, "it is better to be able to control your passions than to command a whole army." God has given us the fruit of the spirit of temperance (self- control), but if we allow satan to dominate our feelings and emotions, defeat is inevitable. Beloved, we must renew our minds on the God's Word. We must live out of our spirit man and not be dominated by our feelings and fleshly emotions. While man is an emotional being we must allow our love of God and faith in Him to influence our actions. God wants us to express emotions in our human relationships in accordance to His love nature. Jesus is our example how we ought to respond to betrayal, unforgiveness, malice and emotional trauma at the hands of others (I Peter 2:21-25 and Romans 12:17-21). Responding and modeling the forgiveness of Christ is a process, but it is an obtainable goal. As you renew your mind on the Word of God and give your body as a living sacrifice, your thoughts become His thoughts and your ways become His ways (Isaiah 55:8-11). True believers allow the life of Christ to dominate their spirit, soul and body.

Satan's Diabolical Scheme

God declared to satan in Genesis 3, after Adam's fall that He would once again restore fallen man. The promise that the seed of woman would bruise his head, made the devil afraid and nervous (Greek –suntribo crush to pieces, utterly defeat, bring to helplessness {Romans 16:20}). However, the who, what, when and where were never revealed to him. It was at this moment that satan'a hatred for God's creation grew and intensified. The battle was on!

Satan did not know who this promised deliverer was or how God would use this man (who in the Garden showed the propensity for failure). Satan was worried and scared of God's redemptive plan in which He would use a common man to destroy his works. Prophecy after prophecy spoke of a Redeemer, a Savior and a Messiah. As God searched for an obedient servant to channel His will through to bring about His inevitable plan of salvation, satan sought to thwart the willingness of man and stop God's plan. But he (satan) had no clue who God would ultimately use.

In Egypt men were used as satan's pawns in his diabolical scheme to stop God's plans to use the Jewish race - His chosen ones. You see, it was determined that through Abraham the Jews were God's chosen people by which the Messiah would come. When the prophecy reached the ears of Pharaoh that a king and deliverer was to be born of the Hebrews slaves and threaten his lordship, he was determined to put him to death. Satan knew that this deliverer would be one who would be a promoter of the One True God. Operating as satan's tool, Pharaoh did not know who the child was so in fear he sent out a royal decree that all males two years and younger should be killed (Exodus 1:15-22). The attempt was to kill the promised one, Moses.

You see, if satan knew and could identify the household of Amram in which the Messiah would be born, he could have saved the lives of thousands of Hebrew babies by sending the slaughterers to that one particular house, thus spoiling the plans of a Promised Messiah and deliverer.

We must understand that satan does not care who he uses to destroy God's plan in your life. He will use a divorce, untimely death or sexual assault to an innocent child. Do you see who/what we are dealing with? *Hold that thought*!!!!!!!!!!

During the days of Mary and Joseph a prophecy of Isaiah 9:6-7 was about to come to past. He had declared that a virgin birth would usher in the fulfilled prophecy of a Messiah, Emmanuel and a King would be born. Again satan's reign over the lives of men was threatened and he knew he had to stop it. However, he had the same problem as he had in Egypt with Moses – he did not have insight to who God was going to use. Satan was on a mission again using Herod, the tetrarch (Matthew 2:-18). Herod gave command that all male children two years and under to be put to death. Therefore, there would be no promised Messiah to rescue man from his pending sorrows. Satan did not know that God's plan was far reaching beyond an earthly kingdom.

God was ahead of satan every step of the way and warned Joseph to take his bride and son to flee the region. Joseph and his family fled to Egypt as God told him to stay there until otherwise instructed. Satan once again caused the slaughter of innocent lives to accomplish his plan. God was showing his omnipresent, omniscient and omnipotent character in that His redemptive plan would come to past despite satan's attempt to intervene and destroy the Christ child.

You may ask, "What do these stories have to do with my wounded spirit?" It has everything to do with your birth, life and God's purpose for you. Make no mistake about it, satan hates you. He cannot kill you without your permission so he tries to destroy your purpose by causing unfortunate circumstances to happen in your life.

You see, satan knows that God has a plan for your life. He does not know what that plan might be but he knows that purpose spells death and destruction to his kingdom of darkness. Since he does not know what God is planning to use you for to upset his kingdom, he sends death to your home just like he did to Moses and Jesus' home.

However, death comes into our homes while we are infants or children growing in our formal years in the form of divorcing parents, abuse (physical or sexual), sickness/disease, spiritual darkness, poverty or lack. He causes children to be born to ungodly parents that have fought and strayed away from God. Satan uses lies and deceptions and causes parents to fail to protect their children from incest, rape or other sexual perversions. One could be a victim of child molestation or be a child born as a victim of a sex crime. *Satan does not care.* As long as he can manipulate the circumstance of an unfortunate beginning and cause that individual to curse and blame God; he has accomplished his objective.

Satan does not want you to fulfill your God given purpose. He tried to snuff out your spiritual life before you can begin. While I was dying of pneumonia at the age of 9, my mother prayed, "God if you let him live, I'll give him back to you." That simple prayer saved my life and set me on a course that would lead to the ministry of Jesus that I trust the Lord to fulfill in my life daily.

This is why people need to understand that it is important who you marry and establish right relationships in this life. The man God ordained for you to marry might be the union in which He plans to birth the next Billy Graham. A man/woman that God wants to use to warn of the antichrist and turn the hearts of millions to the Lord might be your son or daughter. But if you marry the wrong one, satan will manipulate this situation (marriage) to sow seeds of divorce, incest or spiritual ruin to his advantage.

Satan's plan is simple! *Injure the heart and spoil the plan of God for that life*. Satan has many casualties on the road of life that have shunned God's instruction and yielded to the sins of the flesh (I John 2:15-17). If he can't kill you in the womb, he will kill you spiritually so that you will never find the will of God for your life and never become a deliverer, savior or comforter for others. He was not able to defeat the plan of God for Moses or

Jesus and he doesn't have to destroy your purpose. Allow God to give you victory over your injurious and wounded past. The alternative is to have a death-laden life void of the power of God.

The Ills of Life

"What doesn't kill you will make you stronger"

Society presents difficulties on every hand. Millions are victims of the carelessness and thoughtlessness of others who were sworn to protect, but rather were too selfish. Too often God is blamed for the calamities of life when it was the failure of individuals to include God in their plans. Satan is the source of all pain and suffering, but human reasoning says everything; *good or bad comes from God* (not so - Acts 10:38 and James 1:17). While God may permit evil, He is a good God that wants to be involved in the lives of men.

God permitted the evil that happened to Job, but He did not cause it. Proverbs 19:3 says, "A man may ruin his chances by his own foolishness and then blames it on the Lord" (Living Bible translation). It is God who waits patiently for an invitation from us to intervene in our circumstances. While life might deal you a bad hand to play, God has predestined that you have a winning hand in life through faith in the Name of Jesus. God's plan for you is an abundant life of wholeness, soundness and peace {salvation in the Name of Jesus – Romans 10:13 and Acts 4:12}.

So there will be no mistake about it I want to list some of the ills of life that befall the lives of men/women. Satan has left an untold populous of road kill on the highway of life. Consider the lives left victims to and not limited to the following:

Divorce   Child abuse   Substance abuse
Terminal   Sickness   Sucide   Single   Parenting
Financial ruin   Incarceration   Mental Illiness
Racism   Abortion   Betrayal   Exploitation
Incarceration Repressed memories Racism
Unwanted Pregnancy
Your personal pain   (Fill in the blank)

You may have been a victim of the aforementioned travesties of life. You were a victim or you could have been the perpetrator; regardless, God is able to make all grace abound to you. In life we have no say so to whom we are born to or where we will live. We had no control over our ethnicity or our physical makeup (gender). However, as life unfolds and we began to develop through our childhood, those that were sworn to protect us and provide for us may have been careless and thoughtless in their obligations to provide for us. Our parent or guardians may have been the victims themselves of situation beyond their control. *We suffer because they failed to trust in God.* Our parents/guardians may not have known the saving grace of God and therefore satan may have stolen, killed and destroyed the hope offered by God, Himself.

The ills of life come to us all. Just like satan brought sin and death at the door of Moses' parents or his plot to kill the promised child, Jesus. Satan will try to snuff out your life before it begins. He (satan) is merciless and murderous. His hatred of God is expressed through the sufferings he imposes on the live of God's children. He will divide a happy home through divorce, leaving the spirit of poverty to run its course in their life. A divorce which will leave children defenseless, a wife devastated and a life of bitterness towards a departed spouse and that leaves either divorcee pointing to God as the cause. Satan will work his deception through that divorce to create a subsequent second marriage that could cause the children to be victims of further neglect, sexual or physical abuse and inevitably emotional trauma.

NOTE: Some of the negative responses to the ills of life could be and not limited to: Unforgiveness, bitterness, hatred, anger, self-hate, self-mutilation, loss of appetite, depression, isolation and suicide. All these responses further the cause of satan and makes him happy.

As satan further exploits the ills of that broken home, the victim could drift further from God and His Spirit. Un-Forgiveness, anger, bitterness and hatred hinders God's ability to heal and make you whole. Satan the enemy of our souls is a master of using such emotional trauma and making us immune to the grace of God available to us. Thank God that the God of hope will deliver you from the storms of life to give you victory (Jeremiah 29:11 – NIV translation). *Keep reading if you want to hear about the promises of God.*

The Sins of the Fathers
"You can't unscramble eggs"

Benson Andrew Idahosa (09/11/38 – 03/12/98), was a charismatic preacher and founder of the Church of God Mission International in Benin City, Nigeria. As the First Pentecostal Archbishop in Nigeria he was known for his robust faith in God. However, when I met him in 1988, he told a testimony of abuse, neglect and abandonment. He shared how he was placed on a garbage heap as an infant because his father did not want him. He was a sickly child with a medical condition that caused him to faint frequently. His father ordered his mother to put him out on the house and he was placed on a pile of garbage and was presumed dead.

The love of his mother defied her husband and she brought Benson back into the home as he was crying. The father told his wife that he could stay, but he would not recognize him as his son. For years as a child his father treated him as a family pet and not as one born to him. He would not be allowed to eat at the table with the family. His father would frequently spit on him or kick him when he entered the home.

Despite the emotional trauma of abuse, neglect and rejection, Benson met Jesus Christ at the age of 14 through the ministry of an obedient Christian missionary. Benson grew in the Lord and went on to birth a great ministry that included over 5000 ministers under his apostleship and a ministry school. He went from the derogation of poverty to being hailed as a prince in Africa. He forgave his father and honored him in his lifetime. Benson's life mirrored the life of Joseph (Genesis 37-39) as he overcame all odds and the ills of life by trusting in the God.

Joyce Meyers of Joyce Meyers Ministries in Fenton, Michigan testifies of God miraculous grace and mercy as she survived incest at the hands of her father. Joyce reports that her father molested her most of her childhood and into her adult life. According to Joyce after she was married there were still problems with her father. She reported how the incest affected her intimacy with her husband and how she viewed men for a long time. However, through the grace of God she survived and has a great ministry today. Joyce was able to forgive her father and had the privilege of leading him to the Lord.

As unfortunate as those two stories were, God was able to intervene and get glory out of those lives. We don't have to let our unfortunate past dictate our future. The sins of Benson and Joyce's parent(s) could have ruined their lives forever, but thank God it didn't. We have to make the decision to become victors and not victims. Not to make light of life problems, but I want to say, *"stuff happens."* We must decide whether we are going to go through life carrying the baggage of emotional trauma and wounds (which you aren't equipped to handle) or will you trust God to bring you out. You give satan and people power over you when you _choose_ to carry the weight of that baggage in your life.

You've heard the expression, "everybody has a story." This expression has some validity to it. If we were to sit around and have a pity party, most of us would have a story of some trauma that has left emotional scars and wounds. In many cases, our family has betrayed us or let us down. Some of our family ancestry has stories of abuse, neglect and betrayal that have left its mark on the rest of the family. The lineage of Jesus included thieves, liars, prostitutes or harlots, victims of incest and murderers. No family is without some hidden secrets. The scriptures said, "That love covers a multitude of sin." However, in most families we try to cover up and hide from the sins of our fathers. Proverbs 28:13, says, "He who conceals his sins does not prosper, but whoever confesses and renounces them find mercy." (New International Version) Most of our wounds and trauma is associated with concealing and hiding transgressions. The family refuses to talk about the untimely death, the rape by a trusted family member or loved one, or the betrayal of adultery. The children grow up aware that something is wrong, but the family refuses to talk about it. God can't completely heal the brokenhearted if we fail to confess our sins.

As believers, "old things are past away and all things are new (II Corinthians 5:17), but there needs to be an acknowledgment that we are still broken inside and need God to make us whole. Too many lives are bruised and left black and blue inwardly. They appear to be okay on the outside but a different revelation lies within. Often times those inward bruises make their way to the surface and manifest in the form of hatred, un-forgiveness, bitterness and rejection. Such scars can make it difficult to re-invest in healthy, meaningful relationships or they damage the thought processing making it hard to keep focus. Emotional trauma can work its way to our mind and cause mental illness.

In the case of divorce, partners separate for reasons that are often selfish. The betrayal or the abandonment of marriage vows when children are born to that union leaves wounds that only God can heal. Whether the sin of adultery or the deception of incompatibility is the reason for the divorce, too often the children are the unfortunate carnage and casualties of the breakup. How many times the children blame themselves for the divorce? They feel if they were pretty enough or smart enough; the parents would still be together. The child learns at an early age to feel the pain of rejection, un-forgiveness and unsolicited anger. Again the sins of the fathers have visited the children and caused deep emotional scars. This is nothing more than a wounded spirit that separates a person from his God.

When we as parents duplicate the generational curses of fathers we continue a repetition of sinful acts that leave many wounded. We cannot be in denial, but confront sin and repent. God is able to make all grace abound and heal your broken heart. The blood of Jesus and His Cross is available to every believer that will trust in its power.

Acting out Our Rage

"Two wrongs don't make a Right"

People who have been wounded emotionally will act out. A young girl that is promiscuous and acts out sexually could have been a victim of rape or incest. Often a young man rebelling against authority figures could be a result of an absent father or a victim of physical abuse. He might be a very angry young man because his father left the home. Young girls cutting or mutilating their bodies are suffering from inner pain that is too painful to talk about. Symptoms of delinquent behavior, un-trusting hearts, substance abuse, civil disobedience and failure to connect with others are often ignored when they first surface. Parents or guardians ignore the symptoms until there is full blown breakout of unexplainable behavior that leads them scrambling for a cause. By the time they seek help the issues seem insurmountable and hopeless. Most of their lives, some pastor, counselor or therapist spent too much time treating the symptoms instead of the root cause. (Proverb 26:2)

These professionals in their best efforts have been putting bandages on cancerous sores that have not gotten better but worse. The lady with the issue of blood in the Mark, chapter 5, did not get better by going to the doctor, but rather grew worse. The root cause was that satan had attacked her body with a spirit of infirmity in order that she might suffer rejection and become bitter. Her condition tormented her mentally until death was inevitable. Satan has mastered the ability to use family and trusted family members to leave wounds in our lives that appear incurable (Proverbs 27:6)

There should never be denial or neglect when these symptoms are discovered. The family member that trusts Jesus as their Lord or the pastor desiring to help needs the Lord's discernment and wisdom to delicately administer healing to the wounded person.   Sometimes the pain is hidden behind distrust and misrepresentation of the truth.   As long as satan can hide the brokenness and wounds behind the real cause, healing will never take place.   We must always ask, "Why?"   We should pay attention to the acting out behavior, because behind the negative behavior is a cause.   Too often symptoms or the diagnoses of such cases like ADD or ADHD are treated with medication inappropriately.   The symptoms of substance abuse by the mother is often undetected or revealed in the life of a young child and we label them as ADD or ADHD when the acting out is the result of damages caused in his development in the mother's womb.   It was the parent being irresponsible by using drugs.   The chemical imbalance was caused by the sin of the mother and we are trying to fix behavior with pills instead of compassion and the Spirit of God. Counseling may be available for the child, but the problems go deeper.   The child may be labeled a behavioral problem causing more scars and emotional trauma. God can and will help this child, if somebody will believe God.

FYI: Mothers who have abused drugs before or during their pregnancies or mothers who simply did not want to get pregnant and did, will have children born with the following conditions (remember there other diagnoses): These infants have a high probability to born with birth defects, alcohol syndrome, addictions, autism, detachment disorders, failure to thrive, ADD and ADHD. These infants and children come into the world with problems that make life even more difficult to survive. It increases the propensity for further emotional trauma. If you are a young mother reading this please do not put your child at risk for such things. However, if you were a mother guilty of the before mentioned situations repent and ask God to move on your behalf. I understand that there have been birthing mothers that have had children born with issues and they did not abuse drugs and in such cases the devil is the blame, but God is still able to help you and your child. Amen.

Most of the times when we see unexplainable behavior people may be acting out due to injury that happened years before. *People will act out their pain.* Many people self medicate through substance abuse. A void left by an absent parent may result in anger, bitterness and hatred of self or others. When a child fails to bond with his mother, who was too immature for bearing children, the result could be misplaced affections for any one that shows them attention. Death of a loved and cherish family member often causes people to question God's involvement and His love for them. There is a long list of acting out behavior due to inner pain unresolved. Depression and isolation are not healthy acting out behaviors or diagnoses. You see, there is some acting out behavior that cannot be treated with a pill or incarceration. God needs to be invited to help and deliver the person(s) from an ungodly mindset or stronghold. Some acting out behaviors have greater consequences than others.

When some of those acting out behavior crosses the line of civil disobedience and places others at risk, there are laws that could lead to deeper consequences judicially, leading to incarceration.

Examples of acting out behavior (in children or other family members): Running away, defiance, delinquency, substance abuse, and violence, problems at home (school or community), depression, mental illness, abuse and violence. Look out for changes in eating habits and sleep patterns. Watch loss of appetite, increase in appetite and inability to hold down food. Change is peer group, drastic drop in grades, loss of interest in things that were important to them and social anxiety. If they complain of feeling unloved or lonely don't ignore them.

An Over Medicated Society

"Not a pill for every ill"

In brief I want to share this thought. We live in an over medicated society. Modern technology and sciences have perched themselves on a pedestal observing the wounded in life and set themselves as gods assuming they are the answers to what ails man. They feel they have a pill for every problem of man. While there have been man-made miracle drugs that have soothed the ills of man physically and mentally temporarily, man should not take the credit. However, there is some physical and emotional trauma that only God can heal. And let it be known that there is no pill or medication for the broken heart or a sin sick soul in man. Only Jesus is the mender of broken hearts.

There are those who look to medication to overcome depression, anxiety and worry. Many turn to alcohol or drugs to escape their troubles or evil conscience. Substance abuse of alcohol, prescribed or non-prescribed medication or any other mind altering chemicals might provide temporal or pseudo relief, they can't make one whole after God's design and purpose. Some worship their doctors and aspire to give them praise for saving their lives through their professional advice and assistance. However, it must always be remembered that God deserves all the glory. *While God may heal some through the aide of doctors, God is yet the ultimate source.*

Self medicating has become the norm in human life today. Society has provided a haven for man to escape life's trouble through the solution of drug addiction and other substance abuse. Many adults and teenagers self medicate to silence the voices of despair, hopelessness and emotional pain. The temporal escape afforded by drug abuse is worth manipulation of others and stealing if necessary as individuals cast caution to the wind to be free from their pain. Parents neglect their children, leaving them vulnerable to predators while they seek their next "fix" to get them through the day at hand.

These abusers of drugs learned at an early age to abuse drugs given to them to fix ADD or ADHD symptoms or depression. Since their parents did not know how to trust God, their faith was in medicine or a pill that was supposed to cure them. All this did was teach our children that society has a pill to fix their problems. The child grows up taking medication all their lives and when their parents are no longer there to guide them medically, they will turn to medication (legally or illegally) to fix their problems. In most cases they abuse alcohol or other chemical substances to fix their behaviors or calm their nerves. Abuse of prescribed medication is becoming a growing problem in our society as well. Thousands of teenagers are stealing medication from their parents and are either using them or selling them to others for the purpose of self medication. Satan has deceived people to believe that there is a pill for every ill and instead of calling on the Lord for help they look for solutions in a pill. God help us to break the sin of faith in a medical solution to heal our wounded hearts.

Before you accuse this writer of being against medicine or the mental health profession, let me stop you. We have had great breakthroughs in the name of medicine and mental health and I praise God for that. We have great Christian brethren in those fields that have mixed their training with faith and compassion that has helped heal the lives of many. If it were not for those individuals many Christians would be severely tormented or dead. However, my point is this, that God has already provided answers in His Word that speaks to the wholeness of man: spirit, soul and body. He is not the author of physical and mental illness, but rather He is the healer. Satan is the tormentor that causes depression, anxiety, insomnia, stress, phobias,

ADD, ADHD, schizophrenia, obsessive/compulsive disorders and suicide. Jesus said, "satan came to steal, kill and destroy, but I've come that you might have life and life more abundantly." (John 10:10) My point is that the Word of God preached, believed and acted on will heal any ills of life.

Have you noticed that most mental illness requires daily medications that some have awful side effects? One of those side affects in some psychotic medication is suicide. This plays into satan's hand because you read about it in the news weekly of some emotional disturbed person committing suicide after he has killed others in the process. It would be reported further that he/she was under doctor's care but they don't know what went wrong. *I'll tell you what went wrong; the devil began to whisper in their ear and they surrendered to the devil's power of suggestion to harm themselves and others.* The Bible said that God would give us perfect peace if our mind is

72

stayed on Him (Isaiah 26:3). If you have the peace of God, satan can't tempt you with self harm and suicide. Very few mental health professionals are going to counsel you to trust God and turn to Him in prayer.

God wants you to submit to the help offered by His Good Samaritans (Romans 10:17). Those called to minister His good Word to you are available to you. Let the Good Samaritan lead and direct you to a Bible believing church that will minister to you and get you through the process of God's healing power for your spirit, soul and body. Some may need to go through a process of healing experiences until they are completely whole. Thank God for the professionals in their fields of specified skills of psychiatry. God's ministers who specialize in their fields (internal and spiritual healing) will help you. It is through God's process that will require your obedience and trust in the Cross of Christ. Jesus has already paid the price for your healing so there is no expense to you. You can get through your emotional trauma and walk in freedom. Seek the Lord and ask Him to point you to His Word and His minister(s) who will pray for you to be made whole. Praise God!

Broken Vessels

Psalms 31:12 – "I am forgotten by them as though I were dead." "I have become like broken pottery (vessel)."

The multitude of individuals wounded by life troubles are like broken cisterns that can hold no water (Jeremiah 2:13). No matter how much you love on them and pour in the healing balm of Gilead, the medicine of the spirit spills out on the ground. These individuals need to accept God's grace to heal them completely. The trauma of life has beat them up and left them broken and un-useable. However, God is standing ready to heal them and make them useful again. Until you receive the healing power of God for your brokenness, you will never be effective in ministry at your church, your home or in the community in which you live.

Wounded people lives are filled with cracks and holes that leak out the presence of God. Until they are healed and made whole all efforts are futile (Jermemiah17: 14). Too often those in the ministry and helping professions work tirelessly trying to bandage and restore these broken lives only to witness them rebelling, acting out and fighting the very cure that can heal their broken heart. Don't despair; help is on the way.

People who are broken are sometime incapable of loving others. They usually turn to self-hate behavior. Satan exploits their hurts to make them justify their acts or cause them to blame God. These individuals blame God and others for their pain and instead of turning to God for help they turn and run from Him. Marriages are ruined because people are holding on to pain from a childhood or former marriage. Children act out and are not responsive to God's love because of rejection felt from a father or a mother. Intimacy in a marriage is distorted because a childhood experience with molestation or rape. All these situations caused these individual's lives to be affected and now as adults find it difficult to function in human relationships with others. They must experience the healing power of God or fail in life's precious relational moments.

Jesus tells the story of the Good Samaritan in Luke 10: 30-37, who went the extra mile. The victim was left for dead along a treacherous and dangerous stretch of road. The Good Samaritan picked him up, placed him on his donkey and took him to an inn where his wounds would be further bandaged and cared for. After he had cared for him as long as he could, the Good Samaritan left him in the care of the innkeeper and offered to pay for any additional charges for his care. The man was not to be released until he was totally restored and healed.

Notice in this story of two religious clergy offered no aide because they were void of power and compassion to act on this man's behalf. However, a Samaritan, a half-breed, looked beyond social norms, religious barriers and racism to assist one in need. It was obvious to him that the enemies or thieves had injured this man and left him for dead. He saw an individual made in the similitude of God, suffering and he felt a moral and spiritual responsibility to help (James 3:9). This victim could not help himself so he needed the compassion of Jesus to be shown. So many individuals that are suffering from lives emotional traumas just need a kind word, a smile or a compassionate touch from another human being used of God to be there. If you are a broken vessel you will not be able to administer God's love and compassion. Allow Jesus to heal you and be of benefit to the Kingdom of God.

David said he looked for help, but "no man cared for his soul" (Psalms142:4). These broken vessels, marred by life's trouble are like this man helped by the Good Samaritan. They too need their wounds bandaged and oil and wine of Christ's love poured in. We as humans can only provide temporal aide, but with the power of Christ's love and Spirit in our lives (ministers of Christ) we do not operate as just "mere men" (I Corinthians 3:4 – NIV). God can anoint His ministers to cause them to bring healing words of comfort to you. God wants to grant to all men salvation. The interchangeable words of salvation, saved, made whole and redeemed denotes soundness, wholeness and completeness. As Christians we carry the message of Christ that makes men whole. We are called to lay hands on the sick that they might recover (mend, return to original state). As God's servants we are called to do the works of Christ and perform greater works by the presence of the Holy Spirit in our lives (John 14:12). Therefore, we are called to heal the broken hearted, preach deliverance to the captives, recover the sight to those blind and set at liberty them that are bruised (wounded – Luke 4:18). We are empowered by the Spirit of God and His gifts. As we glorify the Father God we understand that it is not by our power, or might but by His Spirit that works through us (Zechariah 4:6). Through the Gospel message we are to empower the believer to have total faith in God and walk in victory over life's circumstances and storms.

God will not only restore the broken vessels, but fill them with His Spirit. God's spirit will take away the pain caused by the life's trouble. He will teach and empower them to forgive their captive instead of developing a stronghold mentally of hopelessness and despair. Those healed by God will have their joy and peace restored and give testimony of God's power of deliverance (Revelations 12:11). He (God) may have found you bleeding and dying on the Jericho road, but He will pour in the oil and wine to heal your broken soul.

Don't Blame God

It has often been asked, "Why do bad things happen to good people?" In many cases there is never a good answer. Job was a righteous man that feared God and hated evil. Jehoshaphat and Hezekiah were righteous men that had the same character and desire to obey God. You may have had a relative that loved God and went to church every time the doors were opened. Despite their commitment to God they were diagnosed with cancer and died within several months. I must tell you I don't always have an answer in those situations. However, if it is any consolation I want to say, "Don't blame God." While He may have allowed it, *satan and sin is behind it all*. We don't understand the impact of Adam's sin in the Garden and how it had eternal consequences on man.

Thanks to Adam the father of the human race we have an innate habit of blaming others for our failures in life. It was Adam that was quick to blame his wife Eve for his fall (Genesis 3:12). <u>While in some cases we are innocent victims of the mistakes of others, God is not the one to blame</u>. Case in point, you may have been born as a result of your mother being raped by a stranger or family member. You may grow up not knowing your father. Circumstances that surrounded your upbringing were beyond your control. As unfortunate as all those circumstances may be; God never stopped caring. God was there all the time, but you might say, "why didn't God help me?' Did you ever think God led some one to counsel your mother not to have an abortion? I know you have questions, but don't despair I'll get to that; just keep reading.

The scripture is full of individuals whom God loved that suffered at the hands of others. Children were born out of wedlock, orphans in life that were abandoned, bruised and scarred. Gideon asked the question, "If God is God where are all His miracles and why has all these troubles come on us (Judges 6:12, 13). Too often this is the cry of millions. We see all the trouble life has brought and we must blame someone. In the Old Testament, God was blamed for everything; good or bad. They blamed God in ignorance. *Old Testament patriarchs lack spiritual insight due to the limited revelations given to them by God.* God was blamed for Job's troubles. Isaiah 45:7 says, "I form the light and create darkness: I make peace and create evil; I the Lord do all these things. Micah 1:12, "but evil came down from the Lord unto the gate of Jerusalem." Without getting into a theological discussion, let me say that the active Hebrew verb, "create" is in a *permissive sense* and indicates that God "allows or permits" evil. *God only permits evil.* He does not literally create evil. It would be out of His divine character to create (make) evil. He only permits it to come as a result of man's disobedience. It is a process of reaping and sowing.

God is a good God and can only give good things (James 1:17 and Luke 11:7-13).

Nowhere in the New Testament (except for in cases of judgment – Section X – Misunderstanding the Sovereignty of God), *does Jesus blame the Father God for any calamities or troubles.* Jesus does not blame God for untimely deaths and divorces. He even said that it was through the hardness of man's heart that God allowed divorce (Matthew 19:8). We are to live as New Testament saints and while things in the Old Testament were written for our learning and example, we must understand that we are to follow the example of Christ (Romans 15:4). Jesus' recorded words by the apostles and the teachings of Epistles serve as the standards that we ought to follow and give earnest heed to. Read Philippians 4:9, I Timothy 4:12-16 & II Timothy 3:15-17 It is wrong to take one scripture and build a premise on it and not have two or three witnesses from other scriptures to balance out the meaning (II Corinthians 13:1 and II Timothy 2:15).

In Luke 13 – He said that it was because of satan's ability to inflict people with infirmities (the lady that was bounded). Notice He said that she was a daughter of Abraham and deserved to be healed. Jesus said that satan bound her for eighteen years (vs. 10-17). He acknowledged that satan and demon spirits were possessing the man of Gadara (Mark 5:1-20). Jesus told Peter that satan had come upon him and caused him to speak words of unbelief (Matthew 16:22-23). When you read the New Testament we must read it with the understanding that God is not angry with man and that He has presented evidence before and after the death of Christ that shows God reconciling with man through the shed blood of Jesus. *We must filter all our understanding of God in the New Testament and beyond through the eyes of the Cross and its redemptive truths.*

Satan is the author of sin and death (Romans 8:1, 2). God gets blamed for evil and evil acts which He had nothing to do with. Dr. Robert Young, the author of Young's Analytical Concordance to the Bible and an outstanding Hebrew scholar points out in his book, "Hints and Helps to Bible Interpretation"; he says that in Exodus 26:15, the literal Hebrews reads: "I will permit to be put upon thee none of these diseases which I permitted to be brought upon the Egyptians, for I am the Lord that healeth thee." Notice he recognized that sickness was permitted as a result of disobedience, not because God was a cruel, revengeful and non-compassionate God.

Jesus is the healer and satan is the oppressor (Acts 10:38). Satan is the author of death and he has the power of death (Hebrews 2:14). God hates death. So as in death, satan causes sickness, calamities, troubles and heartache. It is God that wants good for you. It was not God's fault that your dad divorced your mother and left you fatherless. God did not orchestrate the circumstances of betrayal and your parents' failure to protect you from incest, sexual perversion or molestation. Satan was behind the birth that left you deformed or born with a disability. Your mother was influenced by satan to abuse drugs that caused your birth defects. Satan institutes and drives maladies in the lives of individuals. Sin is the results of man's demise and the by-product of sin is the unfortunate circumstances of life. James 1:13-16, says that God does not tempt man with evil, but men are drawn away by their own lust. *Jesus came to destroy the works of satan; not encourage them (I John 3:8)*

God said in Deuteronomy 30:19, "I call Heaven and Earth to record this day against you, that I have set before you <u>life and death</u>, blessing and cursing; therefore <u>choose life</u> that both thou and thy seed may live." God's choice for you and I is life. Now if He wants us to choose life then, life and abundant life is God's plan for us. If this is the choice why would He orchestrate calamity and death-filled events in our life? Paul stated that death was the last enemy of man to be conquered (I Corinthians 15:51-57).

Jesus came that we might have life and life more abundantly (John 10:10). God wishes that no one perishes, but enjoy the blessings of life; presently and eternally. He has dealt to every man the measure of faith to grow and mature in order to obtain the promises of God. Despite what may have happened in your life, God's design is that you trust Him. He will heal your broken heart. Jesus came to set you free. God wants you as His own. He wants to heal the damages caused by a cruel devil that seeks your destruction. Many suffer needlessly and endlessly because they refuse to trust God to heal them. Cry out like Jeremiah, "heal me or Lord and I will be healed; save me and I will be saved:

for thou my praise. (Jeremiah 17:14) God is not the cause of your pain so don't blame Him.

Thou Will Be Done

Death; spiritual or physical, has never been the will of God for His creation. Man was originally created to live forever. The result of sin and its consequences produced death (Romans 5:12-17). Even after Adam sinned, God did not kill him. He could not kill His own creation so an animal was killed. Its skins were used to cover man's nakedness. God views death different from man. Man sees death as the end of physical life. God sees death as separation from Him spiritually and being held captive by satan.

In God's redemptive plan we can have life and life more abundantly. We will live forever in the New Heaven and the New Earth. Some of us will die a physical death in this physical body, while our spirit man will live forever in His presence. In this life, physical death is a shortcut to glory. *"For to be absent from this body is to be present with the*

Lord" (II Corinthians 5:8). Regardless, how one dies, God is not the author of death, but of life. Satan has the power of death and God permits it only because of Adam opening the door through sin and transgression. <u>God may be sovereign but when men refuse the intervention of God and trample on His grace, death is inevitable.</u>

Sin is the root cause of sickness that leads to death. Because of sin men violate certain rules of nature and they incur various diseases and cancerous conditions in their bodies. Satan's influence causes divorces, murders, hate crimes, and pre-mature deaths. Sin stops God from intervening in the affairs of man. Jesus came to give you life and not to take it. Most of man's problems are self inflicted as they are caused by their direct disobedience (or the disobedience of another).

Jesus admonished that we pray, "Thy will be done on Earth as it is in Heaven" (Mathew 6:9, 10).

There is no death in Heaven. There is no sickness in Heaven. Where would God get sickness and disease; He is a good God. If death was His will, Lazarus would not have died (John 11) and/or Jairus' daughter would not have died (Mark 5). Jesus said, "I always do those things that please the Father (John 8:29)." If death was God's will Jesus was in disobedience when He raised the dead. If hunger was His will, Jesus would not have fed the thousands (Matthew 14). Jesus would have let the disciples drown by way of the storm (Mark 4), if it were God's will to let man be destroyed. All the promises of God tend to life, health and wellness.

I recently heard a young man on ESPN network being interviewed by a reporter in response to the death of a teammate killed when he fell from the back of a truck following a domestic dispute with his fiancé. He suffered head injuries and trauma which led to his eventually death. He said that his grandmother always told him not to question God about incidents of this nature. He was implying that God took this young man's life. Like so many do, they attribute all deaths to God, no matter how hideous or unfortunate. Satan influenced this young man's death through domestic abuse which could have been avoided. They were not trusting in God and operating in the God-kind of love for their relationship. Satan stole this young man's death prematurely.

How often have I heard at funerals of individuals, no matter how young or old; some misinformed relative or preacher will say, "God was strolling through His Garden and decided to pluck a rose (the deceased). *Not true.* Or they will say, "We loved them, but God loved them best." **What???** God had nothing to do with that. The deceased could have been a young man that wrapped his car around a telephone pole while under the influence of drugs. How did God have anything to do with that?

Surely, He could have taken this young man home with Him without such a tragic death.

God is not in the business of leaving women widows or children fatherless. Although He is married to the widow and the father to the fatherless, <u>He did not **take** your loved one</u>. Through some unfortunate set of circumstance death may have occurred, but if you trace the origin you'll find that satan had a hand in it. God would prefer that we all go the way of the sky and the grave is a second choice. God would prefer we all die in the Lord (being saved – Psalms 116:15). Heaven is a place for prepared people so unless God has prepared that person for death, why would He take them?

"Why destroy yourself? "On the other hand don't be too wicked either – don't be a fool!" "Why should you die before your time?" (Ecclesiastes 7:17 – Living Bible translation) According to this scripture many people (Christian and non-Christian) die premature deaths. Many people expedite their stay on Earth by living riotous and reckless lives. Read Psalms 55:23

A young man is caught up in a street gang and is gunned down at the age of 13. It was the plan of God for his parents to nurture him in the admonition of the Lord. Instead, through sin and selfishness of the parents and subsequent divorce, he is without guidance and direction for his life. He is left bitter, angry and unforgiving. He becomes vulnerable to the streets and the gang offers him a pseudo-family. The young man follows the path of destruction because satan sowed seeds of civil disobedience. The plan of God was for his parents to follow Him and provide a safe haven for the young man. God wanted the parent to give him instructions for a productive life by teaching him God' Word. God is blamed for his untimely death, while satan arrives at the funeral rejoicing that all fingers point to God.

This is the case in many deaths. A grandparent who smoked cigarettes for 70 years was warned of his doctor for many years to quit smoking, but he would not. Cancer racks his body and opened the door to other ailments as a result of the 4000-plus poisons in just one cigarette. You mourn because he dies a slow and painful death in the hospital of lung cancer. You stand helpless as you watch his life slip away. At the funeral your minister talks about his community achievements and legacy he left behind. He talks about his Christian service and faithfulness to God's command of marriage as he and your grandmother were married over 50 years. Some weep, while other mourn and grieve painfully. He concludes his eulogy by saying God called him home to a better place. He might be in a better place, but did God call him home? As a young child you try to understand why God killed grandpa. There is no mention of satan's influence on grandpa's flesh to abuse his body and sin against it by smoking for 70 years. It was God's plan for him to live 80 plus. "With long life will I satisfy you and show you my salvation." Psalms 90:10, 91:16 and Job 5:26). It was the will of God for him to take care of his temple and not smoke (contaminate his body and lungs for 70 years). Had he listened to the Holy Spirit, he would have never smoked all his life.

God has given us wisdom that will sustain and increase our quality of life if we follow His commands. *As long as we are in these fleshly bodies, sin makes us susceptible to illness and death.* Our natural bodies are decaying with time. Under the Old Testament we are subject to 70-plus years to live. With the promises of the New Testament, God could by grace cause us to live longer than that. However, it is up to us to take care of our natural bodies.

Our bodies are the temple of God and we are told not to abuse it. Read First I Corinthians 3:16, 17 and 6:19, 20. Habitual sinning and yielding to various unhealthy vices (smoking, substance abuse, poor dietary practices, etc.) will be judged by God. Death is the result of constant disobedience and over indulgence in hurtful fleshly appetites. Medical science has given us helpful hints that will help us take care of our temple. In the writings of the Law of Moses there were some laws written as healthy eating habits that would prolong life. Today the Holy Spirit will direct us to listen to sound counsel of physicians and doctors that were meant for our learning. There are natural herbs that properly ingested will provide healing to our bodies and prolong life. God created herbs and placed them in the Earth for our benefits. Natural herbs and organic vegetables will provide healing that certain medicines cannot. Use God's wisdom and allow His natural Earth remedies to give increase to your life.

"If any one does hurt to God's temple or corrupts it or destroys it, God will do hurt (or permit) to him and bring him to corruption of death and destroy him (I Corinthians 3:17 – Amplified Bible). Abusing your physical body could lead to an early death. God cannot be held responsible for such deaths. Eat right and get some exercise regularly. I Timothy 4:8 says, "bodily exercise profits a little;" so get some.

It is attention to such small details that is the will of God. His will is that we enjoy life on Earth. God wants us to live fully healthy lives and enjoy some of life's pleasures in godly moderation. He has willed that we use wisdom in the face of trusting Him with our lives. Sometimes the doctors misdiagnose us and could cause great harm if we solely trust their wisdom. God's Word of truth does not change. Seek God and His righteousness and life will be added to you. Matthew 6:

Appointed to Die

Hebrews 9:27 – And as it is <u>appointed</u> unto men <u>once</u> to die, but after this the judgment.

Each of us has an appointment with death. Some will go the way of the grave and some by way of resurrection (I Thessalonians 4:13-18). Unless Jesus tarries we will all face death. But we don't need to arrive at that appointment one second too early and we definitely will not be one second too late. While others rush their appointment by riotous and reckless living, we that serve the Lord should not fear death's appointment, but trust in the living Lord. David said that death is so close and imminent it is only a step away (I Samuel 20:3).

It is not about God calling your number or Him taking your life in a tragic car crash, but rather a divine decree being promised to every man and after that God will judge them. It is about living a righteous life that is pleasing to God and making ready to meet Him. Heaven is a prepared place for prepared people (John 14:1-6). As in the case with Hezekiah (II Kings 20:1-11), who was a righteous king with a perfect heart. However, God warned him to get his house in order or he would die. Hezekiah repented and God added to his life fifteen years. This is a case of an appointment with death being cancelled for the divine purpose of God. However, others have died because they refused to repent or obey the will of God. Ananias and Sapphira lost their lives because of lying to the Holy Ghost (Acts 5). Herod died because he tried to steal God's glory (Acts 12:20-23). In both cases these people rushed their appointment with death. The key to a long life is to live a holy and righteous life before God.

Paul understood that he had an appointment with death. However, Paul said that he had finished his course and that he kept the faith (II Timothy 4:7, 8).

While you are on the Earth, do all that God has told you to do and then you will be ready for your appointment with death. Most Christians are not ready to die because they know that they have not lived a life pleasing to God and that they have not obeyed His plan for their lives. These untimely deaths add to their frustration because they know that they are not ready to meet the Lord. We will be judged by our actions, good or bad; we have to give an account (II Corinthians 5:9, 10). Are you ready for your divine appointment with death?

Unexplainable Deaths

As a minister of God one of the most difficult counseling situation for me is trying to minister to a person(s) that is grieving the death of loved one that was either not sick or who die an unexplainable death. I can never find the appropriate explanation to soothe their pain. It seems that I search for the right answer and nothing that I say calms their troubled mind. All I can do is trust the Lord Jesus to speak peace to their hearts and strengthen them during this time of bereavement.

"These are secrets the Lord your God has not revealed to us" (Deuteronomy 29:29 – Living Bible). The King James Version says, "The secret things belong unto the Lord our God." I will be the first to say that there are some deaths I cannot explain. Some deaths are best explained by saying, "they truly went home to be with the Lord." Why it was His choosing I don't know. It is one of the secret things that belong to God that shall be revealed; if not here when we get to Heaven. I know this sounds like a cop out and it does not always soothe the bereaved, but we don't always have answers. However, the key is not to get bitter with God, but grow in the grace and knowledge of our Lord (II Peter 3:18)

Hebrews 11:5 – The Amplified Bible said "Because of faith Enoch was caught up and transferred to Heaven, so that he did not have a glimpse of death; and he was not found because God had translated him." For even before he was taken to Heaven, he received testimony (still on record) that he had pleased and had been satisfactory to God"(Genesis 5:21-24). Now that is the way I would rather go. No pain, sickness or defeat by the circumstances of life. *This is a true example of God taking somebody.* No horrific car accident, long tern illness or dying at the hands of another; just simply going to sleep in the Lord.

Having an appointment with death is at the Lord's choosing. This type of death gives those family members who knew the Lord such a peace that it passes all understanding. The funeral is truly a home-going celebration because you know that they knew the Lord and their work on Earth was done (II Timothy 4:7, 8). There are scores of saints that I have asked God, "why them Lord?" His response to me was, "Why Not?" He went on to say, "they have finished their course and there is laid up for them a crown of righteousness." Sometimes the best message that person could ever preach was preached at their home going services. God has comforted my heart by telling me they were ready to come home.

Let us not challenge God's timing or choice, but accept His will and sovereignty. He will show us if we truly seek His face and inquire of His wisdom in such matters (Jeremiah 33:1-3). Trust that the Father's knows best. In such cases He will give you beauty for ashes and comfort all that mourn (Isaiah 61:1-3).

Misunderstanding the Sovereignty of God

I'm convinced that many Christians have a distorted view of the sovereignty of God and therefore blame God for many of their problems. God is the supreme magistrate of life. He possesses the highest authority without anyone being able to control Him. He is all-knowing (omniscient), all powerful (omnipotent) and everywhere (omnipresent), yet **He chooses** to be involved in the affairs of man. He does not set back and avoid getting involved in the affairs, but He needs our permission to intervene. He chooses to limit Himself to the will of man. If a man chooses to detain God by His stubborn will or disobedience, God has no choice but to let man suffer the consequences of his actions.

He is sovereign. He alone can and does choose to be involved in the affairs of man because He loves us. God's sovereignty is subject to His Word. Psalms

110

138:2 says "you have exalted your Word above all your Name." God will not operate outside His promises written in His Word. His blessings and the curses of man have already been established in His Word. Satan and the results of sin will dominate the affairs of men unless they invite God to intervene. Read Deuteronomy 28 [it includes the blessings and the curses upon man's obedience or disobedience.

When man refuses to involve God in his affairs and circumstances, He has to stand back and watch man suffer. Although He (God) is sovereign, He had to allow what happened in the Garden. He had already told man (Adam) what His will was for man in the Garden. Man was to subdue it, dominate his domain and replenish the Earth. It was not His will that He intervene. Man was told what the consequences of His actions would be so God could not knock the forbidden fruit out of Eve's hand or stop Adam from biting into it. As a result man

111

would suffer the penalty of spiritual death and separation from God. *If God had overridden man's will, He would be subject to same controlling attitude of satan.*

However, the sovereignty of God chose to make a promise of redemption that would redeem man from spiritual death and bring him in rightful fellowship with Him. Through His sovereign act He sent Jesus to redeem His creation. Now everything that man needed would be provided by faith in the Name of Jesus. The Cross of Calvary would be God's sovereign act that men could receive salvation, healing and deliverance. When men place their faith in the Cross, God would have a legal right to intervene in the affairs of men. His will would provide for all of man's needs and stop satan's destruction on man. God's sovereignty and man's faith in God can change the calamities of life that confront man. Our lives are not left to chance or a "what will be, will be" mentality. No, God will intervene if men will call upon Him in prayer (II Chronicles 7:14, 15).

NOTE: There is different view of God's sovereignty in the New Testament as opposed to the Old Testament. God dealt with man differently in the Old Testament after the record of man's fall. God dealt with man in the Old Testament after the flesh and used carnal things and He spoke through a selective few men/women (Prophets, Kings, Priests and angelic appearances). Every act of God was pointing to the Cross in the Old Testament, as New Testament saints we view everything from the Cross and beyond. God's sovereign acts were meant to bring men to a point of brokenness through laws and outward covenants. In the New Testament, man's circumcision was of his heart (spiritual). God's sovereignty in the Old Testament was predicated on man's obedience to the law and outward acts, but God requires heart devotion from those after the Cross. When God views man today it is through the eyes of the Cross and its redemptive work on men that believed on His Son. In the Old Testament, men were incapable of doing God's will but in the New Testament, He has given us His Holy Spirit and placed His Spirit in our hearts (Ezekiel 36:26-29). We are held to a higher standard due to the indwelling Holy Spirit in us.

Because of God's relationship with man through the Cross of Christ, He cannot deal with man like He did in the Old Testament. He deals with man like His Father did before the Fall. Man is protected from the wrath of God because of Jesus and His redemptive work. His grace covers us and God has to act through the promises established through a new and better covenant (Hebrews 8:6). Jesus acts as our mediator and intercessor in the face of God's sovereignty. The Bible says, "Therefore He is able also to save to the uttermost – completely, perfectly, finally and for all time and eternity – those who come to God through Him, since He is always living to make petition to God and intercede with Him and intervene for them." (Hebrews 7:25) Jesus is constantly praying God's best for us to prevent many calamities from coming our way. He is our front and rear guard from life's troubles. God's sovereign acts are based on the promises He gave us through His Son. Look to the

New Testament for guidance and answers concerning God's sovereignty.

Someone might say, "God can do anything He wants." "He is God, so no one can stop Him". If that is the case, why doesn't He **make** you pay your tithes? Why doesn't He stop your from smoking, lying, fornicating, etc.? God is sovereign, but *He cannot and will not violate your will.* As Supreme Being He chooses not to violate man's will. If He did He would lower Himself to the position of satan. God made you a free moral agent and He will only intervene with your permission. He has given you moral choice. The Ten Commandment was written to govern our morality and man disobeyed. In the New Testament, He has given His Holy Spirit and men still violate their consciences and disobey God.

God gets blamed for divorces when it was the man that followed his own lustful desires. God gets blamed for school shootings, when it was so-called Christians that voted the Bible and prayer out of school. He can't intervene where He is not welcomed. God gets blamed for wars when it is man's greed, hatred and racism that promote wars. Man's sinful nature dominates his evil desires and God will not intrude on his affairs unless man turns to God in repentance (II Chronicles 7:14, 15). God is sovereign, but He will not extend His hand where it is not welcomed. "The wicked shall be turned into hell, and all the nations that forget God." Psalms 9:17

The Bible says, "These people all trusted God and as a result won battles, overthrew kingdoms, ruled their people and received what God had promised them ..., (Hebrew 11:32-38 – Living Bible). As you read about the heroes of faith through chapter 11 of Hebrews you will see how through faith these individuals wrought miracles and God turned their situation around by their faith and trust in God.

Their situations weren't an act of God that came against them, but rather satan trying to destroy the plan of God for their lives. God intervened only when they refused to be defeated or accept defeat. The will of God was already established through a prophetic word spoken and unbelief would cause God's will to fail. God's sovereign acts were manifested only when men/women believed.

Our faith and obedience play a part in our deliverance and victory. Sometimes what happened to us negatively was not a result of what God allowed, but *what we allowed.* Job gave satan permission when he said "the thing I so greatly feared has come upon me" (Job 3:25). Fear opens the door to the devil and closes the door on God and His sovereign acts. Some died not because God willed it, but rather unbelief and disobedience opened the door to satan's destructive acts. *God responds to faith*; not tears, doubts and unbelief. No matter how much you hope something is the will of God, God responds to the faith that knows it is the Will of God. You can only have faith in God where the will of God is known.

God cannot lie (Numbers 23:19 and Titus 1:2). If God said it in His Word it is truth. While the Bible is a true book, everything recorded in not true. Job said "the Lord gives and He takes away," but God didn't say it. This statement is contrary from the truth of God and His promises. There are a lot of statements in scripture ascribed to God, but God didn't say them. Men made statements in ignorance and because they are recorded we feel that God agreed with them. ***People misunderstand sovereignty because they don't rightfully divide the Word of truth.*** Consequently, man misses out on His blessings because they don't know how to appropriate the principles of faith. Faith can only be applied where the will of God is known and made clear.

Nowhere in the New Testament is there a reference to God creating evil. There are several incidents in the New Testament where God's judgment was imposed and men died and were inflicted with illness. The Spirit of God smote Ananias and Sapphira because they lied to the Holy Ghost (Acts 5). Herod was killed because he sought to steal God's glory (Acts 12:20-23). Bar-jesus was stricken with temporal blindness because he tried to hinder the gospel work of Paul (Acts 13:6-12). Because God is holy, He cannot allow wickedness and evil to enter into His kingdom. _There is a judgment of God that will do whatever is necessary to keep evil men from prospering._ He will not allow men to contaminate that which is holy. I have no explanations in such cases and I warn you do not to fall in the hands of an angry God (Hebrews 12:25). There are some things that hold true whether it is Old Testament or New Testament.

Let me say that God reserves the right to use trials and circumstances for His purposes. God has allowed sufferings for the purpose of producing brokenness in our lives. In Deuteronomy 8:1-6, Moses wrote that God used the desert and wilderness experiences to see what was in the people's heart and whether they would serve Him despite their circumstances. God is after our heart's devotion and consecration. He is not as interested in the present state as He is in the final product. In His sovereignty, God will not force you to violate your will, but He will put circumstances before that will bring you to a point of decision making. (I Peter 5:10)

There are some sovereign acts of God that He allows for the glory of God. In John 9:1-7, He told His disciples that no one sinned in order for the man to be born blind, but rather that God might receive the glory for his healing. We may be faced with a circumstance or situation that we don't know why it came upon us, but you can rest assured when you come out of it, God will be glorified. When you are trying to understand the sovereignty of God you will find out that the best commentary on the subject is the Word of God. Men may give their opinions and human reasoning, but if you balance scripture with other scriptures, you will get the divine answer from God Himself. We don't know all the answers, but God does and He admonishes us to call on Him and He will show us things that we know not (Jeremiah 33:1-2).

Religious Betrayal

"So I begged your disciples to cast out the demon, but they couldn't do it." (Mark 9:18 – Living Bible) The Knox Bible translation reads: "but they were powerless." New English Bible: "but they failed". The American Standard Bible: "and they were not able."

Imagine the pain and disappointment this father must have felt. He brought his son, tormented by demons to the church and they failed to help his son. It was not until the **Church** (represented by Jesus) came along and He was able to get the ministry and deliverance he needed. The disciples represented the denominational and traditional church that is void of power. Jesus represented the true Church of God with its gifts and power to meet the needs of a dying world.

Too often people have looked to the religious church for help and have been turned away. The man that fell among thieves and was a victim of pain and suffering and he was denied help by the religious pretenders in the persons of the priest and the Levite (Luke 10:30-37). These men may have had good intentions to help, but they recognized they were void of power to help. *Proverbs 13:12 – "Hope delayed in its realization prostrates or sickens the heart, but when it is realized it comforts and invigorates the body and soul."*

Too many people lose hope and die prematurely. They have placed their hope in a religious system that is careless and prayerless; void of power to aid and give help. This is the reason many are out of church and refuse to attend church or religious services. They attended a church seeking refuge or answers to life's problems and instead they are disappointed by what they find. They are given a bunch of religious rhetoric and nonsense but not the truth. Beloved, get your eyes off of man and focus your eyes on Jesus the Christ. Don't go away; I'll come back to that thought.

While we are to have confidence in God, man's soulish nature has trained us to trust in someone or something label as a social service or helping professional. We are always looking for a tangible resource that we can get into a car and drive to in order to get help. Although our trouble may go deeper than something physical or emotional, it is really a matter of spiritual nature. There are some things only Jesus can fix or attend to. Just like the father in Mark 9 that took his son to the disciples or the lady with the issue of blood went to many physicians and was nothing bettered but grew worse (Mark 5). The lepers sought a religious system to declare them clean (Leviticus 13 & 14 and Luke 17:11-19). At the pool of Bethesda, the man with the infirmity of 38 years was dependent on other impotent folks around him to put him in the water when the angel came down and troubled the water (John 5). Lastly, the lady bowed over for 18 years with a spirit of infirmity was told by a religious system that her she could not get healed on the Sabbath Day, but rather the other six days of the week. The Bible doesn't say why the lady didn't try to come on the other six days. Nor does it say had she come to them on one of those other six days she would have been healed. However, it does say that Jesus commanded her to be "loosed from her infirmity" and she was.

All the before mentioned situations are individuals who may have had misplaced priorities and trust; but the common denominators is that they all had a need in their lives as a result of the calamities of life. Each of these individuals trusted in someone or something else to help them and their hope was delayed by those who promised help and could not deliver. In some cases, the religious system has failed many. Instead of pointing to the Cross they persuaded them to accept their opinions or methods of treatment void of God's power and will.

People are hurting and the one place they should find help is in the church. When the church is defeated and powerless, the people will be defeated and powerless. If the church is full of hurting people it will produce other hurting people. Too many denominational churches are going through the religious calisthenics of the Bible rhetoric without the Spirit of God. They mention God in their sermons and messages, but He is not in their living. The church is run by religious zealots that do not have empowerment of God's artillery at hand. The people come Sunday after Sunday and sit as God's people, but are not His people (Ezekiel 33:30-33). Jesus told the religious people that their traditions and customs made the Word of God of little affect (mark 7:5-13).

It is not the will of God for people to come to a local church weekly and not get their needs met (spiritually, physically and emotionally). God has given us (Church) gifts to minister to the needs of His people. When that religious system or pastor turns a deafening ear to the Word of God, the people suffer. **I call this religious betrayal.** The Bible talks about pure religion that is undefiled that seeks meeting the needs of orphans and widows {anyone that Jesus has died for also}. The Church ought to be a need meeting organization that turns no one away empty handed.

Many people are confused about the acts of God and His sovereignty because the church has painted two distorted views of God. Some paint a picture of a sugar daddy God that gives us good things with no requirements of personal holiness. Another church paints a picture of a cruel, angry God that punishes us for everything. God is blamed for the calamities of life, labeled as acts of God. Those who trusted in

God are confused and divided in their faith because they have not been instructed properly in the Word of God.

The people come to us for answers and if the head (pastor) of the local church is misinformed and those he commissions to teach are unclear about God's will then the people will suffer. Congregants are like sheep. Sheep need direction. If the head does not teach healing is God's will, the sheep will die premature deaths. If the sheep aren't taught that God will heal their broken hearts and bind up their wounds, the people will be weak, unforgiving and bitter. The sheep will cancel out the power of God and they will be ineffective in their ability to breed other sheep.

The sheep must be instructed that Jesus came to set them free. The sheep have to be shown a more excellent way by the power and anointing of God. The sheep must understand that God is not angry with them but rather loves them and seeks their deliverance. The sheep must be warned about wolves, lions and bears that seek to destroy them and take their lives. Instruct the sheep that death, murder and slaughter come from the wolves, and not God. Show the sheep the devices, manipulations and entrapments of the wolves that may appear as God (religion), but inwardly are murderous and seek to feast on them (Matthew 7:15). Satan has cleverly concealed and hid himself, so that all calamities and destruction are from the hand of un-loving God that does not care.

Satan continues to pour salt in our wounds left by death, divorce, illness and betrayal. Many are angry with God. *They feel that the church betrayed them* Satan masterfully got them to get their eyes off of God and focus on their pain and sufferings. Jesus has shown us a better way. He came to heal the broken hearted and set the captives free. He has provided answers in our confusion and peace in the midst of our storms. While the church may have abandoned us, He has said we are not alone (John 14:18, 16:32, 33 and Hebrews 13:5). The disciple Judas betrayed Jesus, but He never stopped loving him and seeking his restoration. It is not the divine nature of Jesus to betray you. He is a friend that sticks closer than a brother (Proverbs 18:24).

Consider what David said in Psalms 55:12-14 – "It was not an enemy who taunted me – then I could have borne it; I could have escaped. But it was you, a man like myself, my companion and my friend. What fellowship we had; what wonderful discussions as we walked together to the Temple of the Lord on holy days." (Living Bible)   David spoke here of his chief counselor, Ahithophel, who betrayed him.   However, Ahithophel had a hidden agenda because Bathsheba was his granddaughter of whom David had her husband, Uriah killed in order to be with her. His motivation may have or may not have been justified, but what we have is David's trusted counselor plotting with his son to have him dethroned and eventually killed. What betrayal.

The point I'm trying to make is that in David's mind, Ahitophel was his friend. He said that if an enemy would have attacked him, he would have prepared himself. But since it was a person he trusted the betrayal was much more painful. When we are hurt by those we trust we have a tendency to be affected more severely and take it more personal. David said he and Athitophel had gone to church together and had sweet fellowship and communion with each other. He did not see this coming. Although David sinned against him, he underestimated the damage he had done to Athitophel. People can love you and still hold limited forgiveness for your transgression. David crossed the line and initiated Athitophel's actions. However, remember, two wrongs don't make a right! Betrayal has consequences. Athitophel played judge and jury and looked for an opportune time to spring his revengeful trap. This type betrayal is never accepted by God and will never be rewarded. Athitophel committed suicide in the end and never enjoyed a life of peace and forgiveness (II Samuel 17:23).

We have this type of betrayal all the time in the religious arena that leave many Christians wounded and confused. Wounded believers may have shared intimate details of their life with a system that failed to minister to their needs. Athitophel should have been ministering to Absalom (David's son) about forgiveness. According to scripture his counsel was *"as though it had come directly from the mouth of God."* (II Samuel 16:23b) Instead, he took his place as the Judas Iscariot of the Old Testament. When the church does not give you counsel on how to deal with those that have offended you, **this is religious betrayal**. It is the position of the ministers of God to instruct you how to forgive those that are closest to you; brethren in the church. If they do not instruct you in the Word of God, you have been set up for failure and the enemy gets an upper hand. Paul told the Church of Corinth that if they did not properly restore the brother caught in adultery with his stepmother, that satan could gain an advantage over them (II Corinthians 3-11). Although each individual is responsible for his/her own personal holiness and purity, the Bible says that God's people are destroyed for the lack of knowledge (Hosea 4:6). Pastors, teach your people about forgiveness and how to walk in the love of God (Jeremiah 3:15). Offenses are going to come (Luke 17:1, 2), but we have to teach them how to handle them. If we don't teach them, we are betraying their trust in us. Sheep have to be led and we need to have them follow us in our examples of loving the Father and loving others (Hosea 4:9 & Isaiah 24:2 – as the priest {leaders} so are the people).

Victim by Choice; Victor by Divine Providence

"Now thanks be unto God which always causes us
to triumph through Christ"
II Corinthians 2:14

God ordained that Paul should stand before Caesar and declare that Christ was the Lord. However, along the way his journey was met with much calamity and tumults. Life's journey is met with many trials and tribulations. Scripture says, "We must through much tribulation enter into the Kingdom of God" (Acts 14:22). Paul may have had much promise in his upbringing and rearing as a child into his adult life, but truly his real life began when he was converted (Philippians 3:3-8 & I John 5:11, 12).

God's divine providence for his life was to reveal Christ His Son in him that he might preach Him among the heathen nations. Paul was called to preach while in his mother's womb (Galatians 1:11-

16). Despite fortune and fame, political or religious status, high or lows; Paul was ordained to preach the gospel. God has predestined by divine providence that Christ be found in us and we be conformed to the image of God's Son (Romans 8:29, 30). Before the foundations of the world He has chosen that we should be in Him blameless and holy through the eyes of His love (Ephesians 1:4). God has ordained that we be more than conquerors in Christ Jesus and we overcome life's problems through faith (Romans 8:37, I John 5:4 and Revelation 12:11). *Your victory is by divine providence.* We, as Christians, do not live to get the victory, but we live from a place of victory in Christ (Romans 5:17).

Paul was walking by the will of God in Acts 27. Through his life and ministry he suffered many things for the cause of Christ (II Corinthians 11:23-27). In Acts 27, Paul escaped the "perfect storm" by God's divine providence. Although Paul warned the men (masters of the ship) that they should not leave Crete (avoiding the storms; harms) they would not listen. Paul and others were hit by a storm called Euroclydon that was meant to destroy them. God had ordained victory so Paul and his travelers survived as the angel by the Word of Wisdom spoke (verses 21-26). Paul praised God for the victory and was content to be alive as they were cast on the island called Melita.

As Paul was gathering sticks, operating in the ministry of a servant he was bitten by a viper. Usually trials and circumstances occur as we are minding our own business performing the will of God. *Paul could have chosen the attitude of a victor or a victim.* He could have complained like many and said, "If it ain't one thing, it is another." "Why won't the devil just leave me alone?" Too many Christians give up in the battle and quit when victory is around the corner. The viper represented the calamities of life that befall each of us. The viper might represent a bad divorce, financial trouble, untimely death of a loved one, abuse, rape, being fatherless or any number of emotional scars. *The choice of being viewed as a victim or victor is yours. Victimization is a matter of perception.* Some see the glass half empty or some see it half full? If so, did you choose the bad half or the good half?

Paul took the attitude of a victor. Instead of dwelling on the attacks of satan look at the divine providence of God. Paul said within himself, God didn't bring me this far to die at the hand of some venomous viper (satan). Paul shook off the viper in the fire and felt no harm (Acts 28:1-7). By all indications his enemies said he *should have swollen or fallen down dead suddenly,* but they didn't know the God Paul served. When you know your God, you will be strong and perform miraculous exploits (Daniel 11:30). King Darius was expecting Daniel to eaten by the lions, but instead God used them as a pillow for Daniel to rest (Daniel 6). The three Hebrew boys escaped the fire that was heated seven times as hot, without stench of a smoke smell on them (Daniel 3). While others gaze upon you and feel that life's circumstances should destroy you, God has bigger and better plans for you. He wants to turn your test into a testimony of His deliverance and saving power.

Consider the life of Esther. She went from being an orphan to a deliverer of a nation. Ruth went from being a widow to a princess. Joseph was delivered from the dark pit to become a prince in the palace. Rahab went from being a disregarded prostitute to the royal ancestry of Jesus. You don't have to let your past dictate your future. God takes the foolish things of the world to confuse the wise (I Corinthians 1:26-29). God can take nothing (someone considered nobody) and make them great. Don't settle for mediocrity and/or failure when God has ordained victory for you.

You might say, "Preacher, I'm not like the heroes of faith listed in Hebrews 11." "God does not understand my situation or pain." Need I remind you of the pain God felt when He gave His only Son? Or should I remind you of Jesus on the Cross being made sin for you and I and being separated for the first time from His Father? Or the agony God feels when we reject His love to live selfishly and sinfully. God knows your pain (Hebrews 4:15). God sees your pain and His Son identified with your pain in the Garden of Gethsemane and at Calvary. God hates what satan has done in your life. He stood and watched as satan took apart Job's life, but He was confident in Job's righteous faith and integrity and He knew that he would prevail. God is confident if you trust Him, you will prevail in this life by His Son Christ Jesus (Romans 5:17 and Romans 1:17)

The choice is yours. You can let the attack of the viper cause you to view yourself as a victim or a victor. Amos said that he eluded the lion and then he was met by a bear. He said he finally got home; a place of refuge and sanctuary and he leaned on the wall and a serpent bit him (Amos 5:19). The old folks say, "If it isn't one thing it is another" (previously quoted). In some instances that may be true. However, God's Word says. "In all these things we are more than conquerors" (Romans 8:37). Life provides the vipers (the circumstances of life), but you choose to be the victim or the victor. (I John 5:4)

Just Get Over It

"When life gives you lemons, make lemonade"

Sometimes the statement, "Just Get Over It" is used insensitively to those in pain. Those that have not gone through the horrific ordeal that you experienced can't identify with your pain and suffering. They weren't there to witness the emotional trauma brought upon you and it is easy for an outsider to say, "Just Get Over It."

The sleepless nights and burden you carry daily appears unbearable. Thoughts of suicide have hammered your mind constantly. Suicide, as selfish as it is, seems to be the only way to escape your misery and pain. To have someone come up to you and say, "Just Get Over It" makes you angry. Trust me, I've been there. It is easier to say to them, "you don't know what I've been through so don't tell me to "Just Get Over It." "Please let me soak in my pain and misery." "It's my pity party and I can cry if I want to." Your pain is real. Your emotional trauma is real. So why don't people understand.

Beloved, having been on that side of the fence and in that position, I've learned that there is truth to that statement, "Just Get Over It." If I really want freedom in my life I have to come to a place where I have to put the offense behind me and move on. God told the Prophet Samuel to get over the death of Saul and to anoint David as King of Israel (I Samuel 16:1-7). The Apostle Paul said that we have to, as Christians forget the thing behind us (victories and defeats) and press on in God (Philippians 3:13, 14). *Moving on in God is not denial that the incident(s) did not happen but it is acknowledging God's power that kept us from falling completely under satan's control.*

Too often we nurse the traumatic experiences and keep them warm and before us constantly. We don't curse it as being an attack from satan. We must recognize it as satan's attempt to destroy us. If you don't curse it, but rather rehearse it over and over again in your minds you will never reverse the affects of it on your life. Satan wants to afflict your mind and soul in order to steal your peace. As a Christian we must see God through our pain. We must trust Him to come to our help and give us strength. II Corinthians 12:9-12, says His grace is sufficient to get us through it. In our weakness He makes us strong. *He is not the cause of your pain but He is the healer.*

You must get over it! When I say get over it, I'm not saying you forget it altogether, but the pain of it is not there anymore. When you refuse to forgive those that have wronged you, you give them power over you. Usually as you go through your private pain those that have sinned against you continue with their lives while you are stuck emotionally on an emotional treadmill going nowhere. Don't give the devil the pleasure; allow God to heal you and live. The greatest revenge against satan and those that hurt your is to live an abundant life.

If you don't get over it you will have a tendency to hang your hat on every failure in your life on that one incident. Too many young men in prison are blaming their life of crime on the fact that they grew up without a father. A young lady says her life of promiscuity was because she was molested as a child. A woman refuses to marry again but rather habitually shacks up with other men because she learned not to trust due to an ugly divorce. A man says he is a drug addict because he could not handle life's struggles. Each case has some legitimacy, but they are mere excuses in the face of God. Satan wants you to play the 'blame game,' instead of accepting responsibility for your actions. I don't doubt that people are widows, orphans, victims of a sex crime, battered, bruised or traumatized by many of life's problems. My argument is how long will

you let your past dictate your future? ***Get over It
!!!!!***

Joseph was thrown in a pit by his brothers because
they were jealous over what God told him. He was
falsely accused of rape and imprisoned unjustly.
Joseph was counted as dead and yet he lived to
restore and redeem his father's house. Even in
prison for a crime he didn't commit he was faithful
and loyal to God and to those in authority. God can
only promote you from your pain when you make
the decision not to nurse the pain but rather curse it
and not rehearse it. Joseph got over it because he
trusted in God to deliver him from a wounded spirit.
What are you holding on to? How many have you
repeatedly told your story to that could not help
you? Who have you blamed or hurt because you
chose to live by your feeling? Where are you
hanging your failure hat? Are you hanging out in a
graveyard of broken promises or the field of
hopelessness?

John 5 – this man hung out by the pool of Bethesda for 38 years with other impotent folks that could not help him. They were all seeking help and waiting for that magical moment when the angel would come down and trouble the water. This is the case with many of us that register our complaint to people who can do nothing for us. Too often our peer group includes other wounded people who will not tell us what God said but rather say those things that justify our wrongful thoughts and actions. Sometimes our peers are angry with God and blame Him just as you do. The old saying, "misery loves company" fit us in this case. You will never get over it while you consort with others who are not trusting God and know not God.

To *Get Over It,* you have to see it from God's perspective. His Son was on this Earth thirty three and a half years (33 ½) and He experienced every type of physical, emotional and spiritual pain

147

possible. Not once did Jesus blame God or sought to have a pity party. His eyes were ever on His Father. Christ in His humanity was tempted in every area, yet He did not sin. He was our example to follow whether injury came at the hands of loved ones, the church or strangers (I Peter 2:21-25). If we master the love walk of Jesus, the process of walking out God's healing grace in our lives would bring us to completion in Him.

The Healing Process

Jeremiah 17:14 – Heal me, O Lord and I shall be healed; save me, and I shall be saved: for thou art my praise.

There are times in our life that God will instantly heal our wounded spirits if we believe. However, for many the healing of emotional trauma is a process. The scripture asks, "but a wounded spirit who can bear?" (Proverbs 18:14) The spirit of man is the core of his existence and once it is torn or broken the repair takes a process of God working with man to restore the total man (spirit, soul and body). David referred to the Lord as his Shepherd that restores his soul (Psalms 23:1-6).

The word *spirit* in the Hebrew (ruwach) is interchangeable with the word *soul*. Therefore we are dealing with the emotional seat of man (the heart of man). Our emotions are entwined into our spirit man and if we aren't careful we will be dominated by our emotions and not the Spirit of God. See references to the chapter, "Not Built For This."

Once you understand who the thief is that stole your dreams and hopes the process can begin. We must first tag satan as the root cause for the calamities that brought injury into your life. Get your eyes off of your inability to help yourself and recognize it is God that heals the broken hearted. Let the healing begin.

For some the healing process can be instantaneous and for some it is a long and rewarding process. God is willing to walk with you through the healing process. The Good Samaritan in Luke 10, stayed with the man as he mended from his injuries. God will send certain individuals into your life to help you recover from your injuries.

I want to give you several steps that you must incorporate into your life to be healed of a wounded spirit.

1. **Pray** – "If I regard iniquity in my heart; the Lord will not hear me" (Psalms 66:18). "Search me O God and know my heart; try me and know my thoughts. And see if there be any wicked way in me and lead me in the way everlasting" (Psalms 139:23, 24). First pray and ask God to reveal to you if you are unforgiving or harboring injury against someone. If so, repent. Ask for His strength to forgive others so your prayers will not be hindered. Be sincere and honest. If you are hurt, admit it and repent. Allow God to restore you to a point of fellowship with Him.

2. **Look to Your God** – Hebrews 12:2 said, "Looking to Jesus, the author and the finisher of your faith". You must get a

glimpse at the awesomeness of God. God, who created you, is such a great and compassionate God has brought you through that situation and spared your life. Though you might be injured and wounded you're still standing. You are still a candidate for God's saving and delivering power. He still wants to heal you. God is bigger than the situation you are facing. He lives in you and will elevate you over the circumstances through your faith. Appreciate all that He has given you. Now you are ready to stand against any other attacks that satan brings your way.

3. **Forgive yourself** – Forgive yourself for blaming God and hating yourself. You must stop blaming God and yourself. You may have made mistakes that made you vulnerable and opened the door to the injuries, but let it go. Stop blaming yourself for your parent' divorce. Stop telling

yourself that you deserved to be raped. You may have contributed to the offense, but now it is time to release yourself from the guilt, condemnation and self hate. This plays into satan's hands and allow him to beat you up emotionally.

Understand that if God forgave you, it is time to forgive yourself. You belong to God and you don't have the right to beat up on God's property (I Corinthians 6:16, 17)

4. **Forgive those that hurt you**. According Matthew 18:23-35, if we don't forgive those that have wronged us, we become satan's captives giving them permission to torment us. Forgiveness is not an option but a command. It is a choice that we must make and not avoid. God has commanded that we forgive one another regardless of the offense. Luke 17:1-5, Ephesians 4:30-32 and Colossians 3:13 are only a few scriptures that tell us to forgive. Mark

11:25, 26, says that if we don't forgive our Heavenly Father will not forgive us. In order for the healing process to be effective we must forgive others. This is not easy because you must forgive in faith. When you make the decision to forgive you give up the right to be judge and jury. Trust God to give you the strength to forgive and release those individuals to God. Let God handle them (Romans 12:17-21).

5. **Pray some more** – "Prayer is the doctor that diagnoses the heart" (E. M. Bounds). As we spend time in prayer to God, He will constantly show us where we are spiritually and emotionally. God will reveal to us if we have forgiven others and whether we are walking in true forgiveness. Prayer strengthens us and empowers us to walk in the healing process He began in our lives. Praying in the Spirit especially allows the love of God to be shed abroad in our hearts

which chases away all fear, pain and injury (Romans 5:5 and I John 4:18). When we truly forgive others we demonstrate the true love of God in our hearts. True biblical and spiritual prayer will change the circumstance and ultimately change us.

As you continue to pray, allow that praying to turn into another level of prayer called worship. Prayer must bring you to a place of acknowledging God as your Deliverer, Savior and Lord. Worship will bring you into the presence of God and He will remove all your pain, sorrow and misery of your broken heart. He will heal you during those seasons of worship and praise. Thank Him for strengthening you to forgive and walk in His freedom. Beloved, pray, worship and give praise.

6. **Re-invest in other healthy relationships** – Don't be like the man at the pool of

Bethesda in John 5. Once you have experienced the healing power of God that healed your wounded spirit, you need to find a new set of friends or associates to fellowship the love God with. The Body of Christ affords us a safe haven to share and discuss our problems and our victories. You don't need to be in association with other bitter and unforgiving people. God wants you to reinvest and develop a nucleus of brethren that continue to strengthen your desire to walk in forgiven and showing mercy to those who have experienced injury in their lives. You don't have to hang out with those that hurt you. Unless God physically reconciles you with them, you are not required to be in their face on a consistent basis. You have reconciled within yourself and it doesn't require you to have fellowship with your abusers. You can love them from a distance and stay at peace with God. God will provide you with His family of believers that will encourage and strengthen you. However, if is a spouse or family member it may present some challenges, but God will give you wisdom on how to handle such situations. Walk in the love of God and He will help you choose yours actions and words carefully.

The reason God wants you to reinvest in healthy relationships is because He wants you to learn to trust people again. You were created by God to be connected to others and when you learn to lovingly commune and fellowship with others it will bring a new dimension of God's love in your life.

7. **Get a revelation of God's love** – Once you get a revelation of God's love your life will change drastically. God is love and He cares about your well-being. *Understanding God's love is threefold: God loving you, you*

loving yourself and you loving others. God will cause you to experience His love towards you and it will make you respond to Him (John 3:16 and Romans 5:8). As you understand God's love for you, He will open your eyes so you can see your value and worth. He makes us righteous and brings us into fellowship with Him. We as Christians should understand as God has forgiven us we should in turn show love for others and forgive them. Although others have wronged us and sinned against us, they too deserve God's love to be expressed to them. God will use us to show His love to others, even if those people are those that have sinned against us.

God's love in us is a powerful force. When you really get a revelation of God's love in your life you will have to change. (Ephesians 3:13-21) We cannot be unforgiving, bitter, hateful or angry when we truly have experienced His love. We must become love of God conscious. We must be conscious of God's love inside us at all times. In I Corinthians 13:4-8, it tells us what God's love is. We must mirror this love in our lives to others and to ourselves. Ephesians 5:1, 2 – says we are to be imitators of God by walking in love. Walking in God's love is not an option, but a command. Love is the divine nature of God expressed in our actions and deeds (I John 2:11-18). We cannot say that we have God's love in us and walk in hatred towards someone. Love will heal the hurts of our wounded spirit and cause us to show our gratefulness through loving others.

8. **Self-talk** – Speaking God's Word over our lives strengthens what we believe has taken place in our lives. In the Book of Psalms 1:1-6, we are told to meditate in God's

Word day and night. One part of meditating on God's Word that many Christians don't do is speaking the Word of God out of your mouth to be heard by you and others. We must confess that we are forgiven and that we have forgiven others. Romans 10:17, says that faith comes by hearing and hearing by the Word of God. As you speak to yourselves the Word of God it will minister to you and build your faith (Ephesians 5:19). Confess boldly that God's love drives your life and you are able to forgive anyone and forbear with those that have wronged you. If you continue to say, I'll never forgive them for what they did to me," *you won't* and satan will hold you in bondage. However, if you say, "By faith, I operate in the love of God and He gives me strength to forgive my enemies." The power of God's love will take that confession and empower you to forgive. Stop saying what the devil wants you to say and say what the Word of God says about the matter.

As part of your self-talk, tell others what God has done for you. The woman in John 4:27-29 was anxious to return to the city to tell others about His forgiveness in her life. The healed leper returned to give praise (Luke 17). God gets the glory when we testify of His love and grace. Tell others how you could have been dead, but Jesus delivered you from death. Let others know that you were on the verge of suicide, but His peace gave you strength to believe in His power to live another day. Give testimony everywhere you go of what God has done. Tell them what satan meant for evil, God turned it around for your good.

Further step by step process (simplified):

1. <u>Recognize the hurt</u>. Identify what it is and be clear who the perpetrators are and the person(s) who hurt you. Recognize the circumstances leading to you being hurt. Sometimes we hold hurts against people who had nothing to do with our injurious pain. You could be bitter with a parent without knowing all the details. Properly point the blame to whom it belongs (even if it is you).

2. <u>Admit that you are hurt</u>. Don't be in denial. Acknowledge that you are hurting. Admit to the harm you may have caused others. Admit the hurt that you have done to yourself. Admit that the divorce devastated you. It is okay to say I'm hurting and I can't move on. Be honest with yourself.

3. Decide to make a change. Decide that you want God's healing and not a pity party. Be courageous enough to confront painful memories. Decide that you want to put this thing behind you. Decide that you will not carry this hurt any longer by God's grace and strength.

4. Share your story. Be willing to share your painful story with someone you trust and who is qualified to help you. The man at the Pool of Bethesda lie daily with others that were in just as much pain and disgust as he was (John 5). As a Christian talk to your pastor or ask him if he could refer you to some other helping professional. Be willing to have prayer to seek God's direction. *You can't keep carrying this pain in your private life.*

5. Confront the demons of your past. This is where the healing process takes an

upward turn. Be willing to disclose in depth your pain or injury. You can't treat it like the big pink elephant in the living room. Don't ignore it but confront it. It will never go away on its own; deal with it. Do some self talk and if necessary write a confrontation letter to the person(s) and ask your pastor (or counselor) to let you read it aloud to them. Say all the painful things you would say to that person if they were present. Afterwards, destroy the letter. However, if the perpetrator is a willing participant in the healing process have them present (along with pastor) and read the letter to them. Please do not allow them to respond at that time. As some point, have the perpetrator respond in the same matter, expressing remorse and asking for forgiveness. It could be a young man reading a hurt letter to his father who was in prison most of his life. The father may be out now and recognizes how his absence affected his son and is willing to have healing and restoration. Let them both address their pain and seek closure. The pastor or a therapist must facilitate this step.

6. Amend/forgive – Make apologies for the negative behavior as a result of their hurts. Make a confession to God about your unforgiving heart and be willing to release those that hurt you. *This is the place where repentance brings healing.* Ask God to help you forgive those that have wronged you. If you are willing to call their names out before the Lord it would take strength from the devil over your life. If the perpetrators are involved, ask them to forgive you for holding hurt feelings against them. *You*

must forgive if you want to be forgiven.
Mark 11:25, 26

7. <u>Open your heart for healing</u>. This is the last step. Open up your heart and let God forgive you. Remove all obstacles that would prevent you from receiving from God. Hosea 10:12 and Jeremiah 4:3 – break up the fallow ground of your heart. Let God pour in the oil and wine of His power to restore you. The Holy Spirit is a perfect gentleman and He will not force His will on you. You have to open up your heart to Him.

Word of Caution to Ministers

(Those that give counsel to wounded victims)

Be careful to avoid the pitfalls of satan that would cause you to be drawn into sin. Too often ministers have fallen into sin while counseling those of the opposite sex. When individuals are dealing with trauma as a result of a wounded spirit they seek out those that show strength, compassion and empathy towards them. This is a natural human response, but as ministers of God we must address these issues with caution. That is why it is important to involve your spouse (or some other individual) in some way. Don't deal with such individuals in a one on one private counseling session. Pastors are extremely vulnerable in these areas and should use wisdom when counseling those who are experiencing emotional trauma. I realize that some one on one sessions may be unavoidable, but as much as possible don't get caught up in questionable situations that could cause the ministry to be evil spoken of.

When counseling a female going through the pain of divorce make sure that you set certain boundaries that would protect each of you from developing a soul-tie that would cause intimate feelings to become mutual. Most women in such cases are looking for a warm embrace or a shoulder to cry on. Women are more emotional than men and more susceptible to bond with their counselor. The male counselor (or anyone of the opposite sex) must not allow himself to listen to the devil and open up a door that would cause their counselee to show affection to them. Once you notice that that the counselee is developing affection and passionate feelings for you then stop the sessions and refer them out to someone else.

We must understand that we are dealing with a formidable opponent, the devil who knows how to manipulate any circumstance to his advantage. If he can work on the emotions of a wounded person, you can find yourself is a situation where they have developed an unhealthy soul-tie with you. You will find yourself in a situation in which the person wants to show their appreciation to you in a sexual way and you would never see it coming. Far too many ministers have fallen into sex sins because they did not pay attention to the warning signs. The Bible said, "Be sober, be vigilant; because your adversary the devil as a roaring lion walketh about, seeking whom he may devour." (I Peter 5:8) He (satan) is good at what he does and if he can manipulate a person's emotions to get them fall in love with you and cause your fall, he will. However, it takes your cooperation so make sure that there is nothing in you that would cause you to cross the line with the counselee (John 14:30). We must all remember that we are responsible for our own personal holiness. Stay pure in your thoughts and in your heart.

You represent a sense of strength and compassion that your counselee aspires to find in their spouse. They are attracted to your passion and strength and desire it deeply. Initially, a carefully placed word of encouragement or a passionate embrace could send the message that the feelings are mutual and before you know it you have a full blown affectionate embrace or even a kiss that could turn ugly. She (he) could start sharing intimate details with you that you don't need to know. Satan will start working on your flesh and cause you to be curious to know more. Just like an obsession of pornography starts with a harmless glance, your drive to know more intimate details could take place and this is not good. You will start fantasizing about that person and soon your thought life will drive you into bondage and an unhealthy soul-tie will develop. You must safeguard yourself in these matters and give satan no place (Ephesians 4:27).

Man of God or Woman of God be prayerful and watch out for any signals that the individual may send that reveal that they have a deep affection for you. Watch out for a lustful spirit that would try to harness your good intentions to help. Never let them cross the barriers of the counselor – counselee relationship. Point them in the direction of Christ and never lose focus of your ministering God's love to them.

Don't develop a Messiah Complex with your counselee. A Messiah Complex is a state of mind in which the individual believes he/she is/or is destined to become that person's savior. You are not the Holy Spirit. You might be the agent that God is using but you don't have all the answers. Don't set yourself as the only one that God can use to minister to that person. Sometimes a person may exalt you above God and look to you, instead of God. The Messiah Complex is dangerous because you are setting yourself above God and making yourself the hand of God. The Messiah Complex, coupled with pride will lead to your destruction. Satan will strategically place a member of the opposite sex in your life to bring you to ruin. Don't be deceived by the trappings of the wicked one. Pray to God for discernment and wisdom to avoid the traps of satan. Ephesians 6:10-18

Conclusion

It is harder to win back the friendship of an offended (injured) brother than to capture a fortified city. His anger shuts you out like iron bars.) Proverbs 18:19 – Living Bible)

Many of us carry the battle scars of life's calamities with us. Wounds that seem to hinder us though most of our lives aren't healed because we won't let things go. Too many Christians are bitter, angry, unforgiving and full of rage. Beloved, this is not the will of God. Harbored hurt feelings and injuries will hinder us from the blessings of God and affect our effectiveness for the kingdom of God. *We will not be able to reach our full potential in Christ if we walk around wounded and unforgiving.*

Solomon says that a person who is injured can put up walls that keep everybody out --- ***even God.*** It is the goal of satan to isolate you from the healing

174

power of God to heal your wounded spirit. Individuals, Christians or non-Christians, can develop a self-hate for themselves and become injurious to themselves. They can feel that God is angry with them and means only bad for them. I've talked to some people that will not even pray to God because they are convinced that He stop listening to them years ago.

"Your words have been strong and hard against Me, says the Lord." "Yet you say, what have we spoken against you?" "You have said, it is useless to serve God; and what profit is it if we keep His ordinances and walk gloomily as if in mourning apparel before the Lord of hosts (Malachi 3:13, 14 – Amplified Bible). There are many who feel it is useless to pray and serve God. They feel God is the cause of their pain. I've had some ask, "Where was God when I was going through my troubles?' "Why didn't He help me?" Satan has been allowed to steal their hope and desire to live for God. This is what he tried to get Job to do, but he was a righteous man that trusted in his God.

Trust me, it was painful for God to watch the situation Job's situation and it is painful for His to watch you go through your situation. However, God was trusting in you to turn to Him and ask for help to deliver and heal you. Many have said, "I prayed night after night and God did not come. Before you say God didn't show up, examine your heart. Did you want God to deliver you His way or your way? *What was your motive and would you forgive those that injured you once God healed you? God's knows your heart and the attitude of your heart will affect God's response to your request.* (Psalms 66:18, 38:18)

A story was told about a man standing on his housetop during a massive flood in his city. Water covered the whole city. He prayed that God would save him while he was standing on his rooftop. As he was *waiting on God*, a boat came by and offered to rescue him. He replied, "No, I'm waiting on God." A helicopter came by to rescue him and he replied again, "No, I'm waiting on God." After a while the water rose further and the man drowned. When he opened his eyes in Heaven, he asked the Lord, "Why didn't you come and save me?" "I called out to you, but you never came." The Lord replied, "I sent angels by twice but you refused My help on both occasions."

This is the case with many wounded people. God has opened doors to provide healing for their wounded spirits but they failed to recognize His provisions. There is counseling available through the local church, trusted friends or the avenue of prayer with and by others. Too often, wounded people reject God's help and die without every experiencing God's salvation. Satan has cut their hearts so deep and has blinded their eyes; they feel they are beyond saving. Rejecting God's healing grace and blaming others is satan's way of keeping them in bondage.

Don't drown in sorrow and misery. Job had more reasons to curse God than anybody in the entirety of the Bible. However, the scripture records, "in all this Job sinned not, nor charged God foolishly." (Job 1:22) Job refused to curse God or blame God for his troubles. He didn't understand it all, but he knew not to blame God. A better translation or interpretation of Job 1:21, should read, "the Lord gave me everything and if He wants to take it away it is up to Him". He did not directly accuse God for losing everything. God commended Job for holding to his integrity (Job 2:3).

Job 42:10 –"Then when Job prayed for his friends, the Lord restored his wealth and happiness" (Living Bible). God turned his situation around after Job prayed for those that falsely accused him and tried to get him to curse God. Forgiveness always opens the floodgates of God's blessing. Matthew 18:23-35 teaches us that if we are unforgiving, we give satan permission to hold us captive and torment us. God has to stand back and watch your suffering because you refuse to forgive. When you have sinned against another don't run from God, but run to Him asking forgiveness.

God is rich in mercy and desires to trade your pain and brokenness for His love and peace. Psalms 34:18 says, "God is near to those of a broken heart and a crushed spirit." He stands with open arms open wide beckoning for you to come to Him to be healed. He does not want you to carry the pain any longer. He needs your permission to heal your wounded spirit. There is an abundant life of peace for your heart and mind in Christ Jesus. There is no more need for mourning, sackcloth and bathing in ashes. Jesus will give you beauty (cheerful anticipation) for those ashes. God will cover you with His beauty and allow others to view His power in your life that now glorifies Him. Amen.

Isaiah 61:1-3 — the Spirit of the Lord God is upon Me, because the Lord has anointed and qualified Me to preach the Gospel of good tiding to the meek, the poor and afflicted; He has sent me to bind up and heal the brokenhearted, to proclaim liberty to the [physical and spiritual] captives, and the opening of the prison and of the eyes to those who are bound (Romans 10:15). To proclaim the acceptable year of the Lord — the year for His favor — and the day of vengeance of our God; to comfort all who mourn. To grant {consolation and joy} to those who mourn in Zion, to give them an ornament — a garland or diadem — **of beauty instead of ashes**, *the oil of joy for mourning, the garment {expressive} of praise instead of a heavy, burdened and failing spirit; that they may be called oaks of righteousness {lofty, strong and magnificent, distinguished for uprightness, justice and right standing with God}, the planting of the Lord, that He may be glorified. (Amplified Bible)*

The goal of God healing your wounded spirit is for you to be healed and go forward and minister His goodness to others. He wants to make you a tree of righteousness so others can come and find strength and shade from the heated pressures of life. Don't disappoint God by allowing your wounded spirit to hinder the great work that God has called you to do. I say to you, "Be healed and set free, In Jesus' Name.

If you would like to contact Pastor Nathaniel Jones for speaking engagements or to order products please use the contact information below.

Preachlife7@cableone.net

918-214-5825

<u>Printed Books</u>
www.newlifepublishing.biz
www.amazon.com